The Commons

The Hoover Institution
gratefully acknowledges
the support of

JOANNE AND JOHAN BLOKKER

on this project.

PHILOSOPHIC REFLECTIONS ON A FREE SOCIETY

The Commons

Its Tragedies and Other Follies

Edited by
Tibor R. Machan

HOOVER INSTITUTION PRESS

Stanford University   Stanford, California

www.hoover.org

Hoover Institution Press Publication No. 484
Copyright © 2001 by the Board of Trustees of the
Leland Stanford Junior University

First printing 2001
07   06   05   04   03   02   01   9   8   7   6   5   4   3   2   1

Manufactured in the United States of America
The paper used in this publication meets the minimum requirements
of American National Standard for Information Sciences—Permanence
of Paper for Printed Library Materials, ANSI Z39.48-1984. ⊚

Library of Congress Cataloging-in-Publication Data
The commons : its tragedies and other follies /
edited by Tibor R. Machan.
        p.   cm. — (Philosophic reflections on a free society)
    Includes bibliographical references and index.
    ISBN 0-8179-9922-1 (alk. paper)
    1. Commons.   2. Natural resources, Communal.   I. Machan,
Tibor R.   II. Series
HD1286 .C65   2001
333.2—dc21   2001024221

I think that one man may be first-rate but if you get one man and two second-rate men together, then he's not going to be first-rate any longer, because the voice of that majority will be a second-rate voice, the behavior of that majority will be second-rate.

WILLIAM FAULKNER

CONTENTS

ACKNOWLEDGMENTS

I WISH TO EXPRESS my gratitude to the Hoover Institution on War, Revolution and Peace, and its director, John Raisian, for supporting the publication of this work. Joanne and Johan Blokker have again given their generous support of the Hoover Institution Press series, Philosophic Reflections on a Free Society, for which I express my deep gratitude. The contributing authors gave their full cooperation, patience, and conscientiousness throughout the entire publishing process. David M. Brown has helped with some editing and I wish to thank him for this, and Jennifer Beattie and Tina Garcia gave valuable administrative assistance. The diligent work of Pat Baker, Ann Wood, and Marshall Blanchard of the Hoover Institution Press is also much appreciated.

CONTRIBUTORS

RANDALL R. DIPERT, professor of philosophy, United States Military Academy, West Point, and C. S. Peirce Professor of American Philosophy, University of Buffalo, is the author of numerous books and articles on logic, American philosophy, the philosophy of mind, and aesthetics, including *Artifacts, Art Works, and Agency* (Temple, 1993).

LESTER H. HUNT, professor of philosophy, University of Wisconsin, Madison, has taught at The Johns Hopkins University, the University of Pittsburgh, and Carnegie Mellon University. He is the author of *Nietzsche and the Origin of Virtue* (Routledge, 1991) and *Character and Culture* (Rowman & Littlefield, 1998).

RONALD F. LIPP, J.D., Yale Law School, 1966, writes on European and American cultural and artistic matters. His most recent publication is "Alphonse Mucha: The Message and the Man." He teaches in the international law program at the McGeorge School of Law, University of the Pacific, Sacramento, California, and conducts a consulting legal practice specializing in American and international antitrust and trade regulation. He is general counsel for the Central California Power Agency.

TIBOR R. MACHAN is Distinguished Fellow and Freedom Communications Professor of Business Ethics and Free Enterprise at the Leatherby Center for Entrepreneurship and Business Ethics, Argyros School of Business and Economics, Chapman University, and a Research Fellow at the Hoover Institution.

JANE S. SHAW, a Senior Associate of PERC (Political Economy Research Center), a nonprofit research organization in Bozeman, Montana, that explores market solutions to environmental problems, is coauthor with Michael Sanera of *Facts, Not Fear: Teaching Children About the Environment* (Regnery, 1999), and coeditor with Ronald D. Utt of *A Guide to Smart Growth: Shattering Myths and Providing Solutions* (Heritage and PERC, 2000).

RICHARD L. STROUP, professor of economics at Montana State University and a Senior Associate of the Political Economy Research Center (PERC), is coauthor with James D. Gwartney and Russell S. Sobel of a leading economics principles text, *Economics: Public and Private Choice* (2000).

The Commons

SOMETIMES, WHEN EVERYONE can get satisfaction, no one can. In his *Politics* Aristotle observed: "For that which is common to the greatest number has the least care bestowed upon it. Every one thinks chiefly of his own, hardly at all of the common interest; and only when he is himself concerned as an individual."[1] Professor Garrett Hardin developed this idea in his well-known essay "The Tragedy of the Commons" (1968).[2] He argued that commonly owned and freely accessible resources tend to become depleted when or if the population exploiting the resources is large enough; for example, a common grazing area that is made available for use to numerous ranchers will be overgrazed and its replenishment neglected.

Communal resources are available to everyone, so everyone has an economic incentive to use them; but no one has an equal incentive to *husband* the resources. The tragedy of the commons occurs because people pursue their goals with the means available to them.

1. Aristotle, *Politics* (1261b30–39).
2. Garrett Hardin, "The Tragedy of the Commons," *Science*, December 13, 1968, pp. 1243–48.

> Picture a pasture open to all. It is to be expected that each herdsman
> will try to keep as many cattle as possible on the commons. Such an
> arrangement may work reasonably satisfactorily for centuries be-
> cause tribal wars, poaching, and disease keep the numbers of both
> man and beast well below the carrying capacity of the land. Finally,
> however, comes the day of reckoning, that is, the day when the
> long-desired goal of social stability becomes a reality. At this point,
> the inherent logic of the commons remorselessly generates tragedy.[3]

Hardin characterizes the "positive utility" to the herdsman of adding an animal to the pasture as something near "+1." The negative
utility would be the cost to him in pasture depletion. Since this cost
is borne not solely by the individual herdsman now adding to the
stock but by *all* the herdsman, the negative utility is only some very
small fraction of "−1." The immediate gain of each increment of
exploitation is thus much greater than the immediate cost, even
though in the end the cost may add up to total ravaging of the
pasture, rendering it effectively unavailable to anyone. This is the
"tragedy."[4]

If the pasture were privately owned and the owner charged for
its use, the situation would be different: the owner would have
every economic incentive to maintain the pasture in order to continue enjoying a profit. The long-run benefit for each herdsman of
continuing availability of the pasture for his use would be worth
the short-run costs. (Hardin believes that Adam Smith is often
wrong to trust the "invisible hand" of market processes as a suitable
allocator of resources, especially with regard to the control of pop-

---

3. Ibid., pp. 1243–44.
4. Hardin quotes Whitehead on the meaning of tragedy as used here: "The
essence of dramatic tragedy is not unhappiness. It resides in the solemnity of the
remorseless working of things. This inevitableness of destiny can only be illustrated in terms of human life by incidents which in fact involve unhappiness. For
it is only by them that the futility of escape can be made evident in the drama."
A. N. Whitehead, *Science and the Modern World* (1925; reprint, New York: Men-
tor, 1948), p. 17.

ulation growth, but he is less persuasive in treating population growth as a necessary instance of the tragedy of the commons than he is in elaborating the tragedy of the commons per se.)

The idea of the tragedy of the commons has been most frequently and fruitfully applied to environmental concerns. Public realms, such as the atmosphere or ocean waters, have seen considerable overuse at the hands of various private parties. In democratic societies the disposition of resources depends on the degree of concern for the resources or for the uses to which they can be put, as expressed at the polls or through the entirely legal process of lobbying and other means by which laws and public policies are influenced.[5] In nondemocratic communities the leadership will favor different goals, some helping and others hurting the public resources at issue.[6]

Various reasons have been suggested to explain why the "commons remorselessly generates tragedy." One frequently mentioned reason is human greed: human beings will always take advantage of free resources beyond what would be wise and prudent. (Less frequently noted is that such imprudent exploitation of the commons, if it can be called imprudent, has often occurred with official sanction if not outright government support.)

Yet it is unnecessary to posit greed or even narrow self-interest in order to understand the tragedy of the commons: merely that people tend to be dedicated to their various projects. If an artist,

---

5. The First Amendment to the United States Constitution affirms "the right of the people . . . to petition the government for a redress of grievances."

6. It is unclear how one can benefit the public as a whole when it comes to particular matters like pollution or resource usage. There are very few things members of the public have in common so they can be hurt or benefited all at once. Not everyone benefits from the same things, and even wildlife preservation or resource conservation may be of value to some but not all. This may explain why some environmentalists have forged a value theory according to which the well-being not of human inhabitants but of nature or earth itself needs to be considered in assessing the merits of public policy.

scientist, merchant, or farmer is given the authority to make use of materials that supposedly all are entitled to use, it will by no means be necessary for such a person to be needlessly and even recklessly eager to gain wealth or other benefits in order to exploit them to the fullest possible extent. It need only be true that the individual or group has serious goals, important projects, or vital causes that can be supported by the resources available to all. Given the belief in legitimate access to the resources in question, the seriousness of the purposes—many of which, individually, are benign and bene-ficial—will generate the tragedy, quite naturally and with no greed necessarily in play at all.

It isn't even the case that people in business, striving to prosper, must be greedy or without conscience in order to exploit public resources such as the air mass, rivers, or forests. When those in business understand that dumping waste into the nearest public river is something they are authorized to do—because, after all, everyone is a member of the public and one's interest is as legiti-mate as another's—they will do so, in the ordinary course of pur-suing their goals. Any professional in business sees these goals as perfectly legitimate: namely, to produce goods and services at the lowest possible cost and to prosper as a result. Such an attitude may be no more than ordinary prudence, exercised vis-à-vis the com-mons without the constraint of definite limits, something provided by malleable public policy.[7]

Nor does a firm that takes its plant to a country with lax environ-mental regulations need to be insidiously motivated. It need only be dedicated to the task of making the business succeed. The mo-tive is no more malign than that of a scholar who is given unlimited use of library resources or a scientist who is provided with large

7. For more on this, see James E. Chesher and Tibor R. Machan, *The Business of Commerce: Examining an Honorable Profession* (Stanford: Hoover Insti-tution Press, 1999).

subsidies. People with serious goals are usually insatiable about the resources that will advance those goals. For merchants to strive to prosper is arguably no less serious a goal than for others to strive to educate or advance human knowledge.[8] The problem of the commons is not that people use the resources to which they have access, but that within that realm there is no appropriate regulatory or coordinating mechanism that enables appropriate husbanding or maintenance of those resources. And in fact, the same "greed" in a noncommunal context generally does not result in the same untrammeled spoliation or depletion.

So we see that when common ownership exists over valuable resources, they will tend to become exhausted. But there is more to the problem of the commons than what is likely to happen with commonly owned natural resources. Not only air, beaches, lakes, rivers, and soil, but anything available for common human use, in fact any task involving common or community effort, is subject to the tragedy of the commons. Whenever decisions are made in common, collectively, inefficiency and confusion tend to proliferate. It can be difficult, sometimes impossible, to determine where the responsibility lies when such decisions misfire. Who is to be held accountable when groups decide?

If members of the group have joined voluntarily, and have a clear goal to pursue, there is a good chance that the terms of joining spell out certain shared responsibilities, as well as responsibilities that vary with individual function. Hierarchies are created by organizational bylaws, partnership agreements, or covenants that specify who is in charge of what area, making possible more responsible conduct by the members of groups than would be the case without a clear chain of command. If ultimate authority is assigned to one particular person, this amounts to the expression of united yet individual decisions.

8. Ibid.

However, there are many groups that are deemed to exist independently of anyone's joining them. Societies, countries, nations, and such are often said to make decisions, pursue goals, and carry out policies, some of which have very serious consequences that may not always be beneficial all around. In such cases, widely evident in politics and international diplomacy, responsibility can become seriously obscured, even impossible to identify. (Who was responsible for the mistaken bombing of the Chinese embassy during the NATO bombing campaign against Belgrade? The pilot who dropped the bomb? The mapmaker whose map provided incorrect information to the pilot? Somebody else, for failing to check the map? President Clinton, for committing the United States to the assault? Congress, for acquiescing in it? The Secretary of State? The American people? My next-door neighbor who supported the NATO policy?)

On a smaller scale we may observe the problem of accountability in the way committees proceed in various organizations (and, more generally, the way any work done in concert proceeds when individual contributions as such are indistinguishable). The difficulty or even impossibility of holding each member directly accountable for the results of his or her input may well contribute to hazy, hasty, poorly considered decisions—or simply to less concern about risks and costs. Indeed, in the name of some larger group or community the members of a decision-making group (say, a government agency or congressional committee) may treat the resources of other individuals, like taxpayers, as a "commons" that they are free to exploit without having to consider costs at all (economic costs are borne by the taxpayers, and any political costs may be very widely diffused). By contrast, the officers of a private company, which must directly bear the cost of any squandered or misallocated resources, have every incentive to structure matters so that even the members of committees are individually accountable (or so that their decisions are far less consequential than those of a very few principals, such as the CEO).

If greed cannot explain the tragedy of the commons, what does explain it? Perhaps the fact that human beings are fundamentally individuals and that their objectives and priorities are not usually interchangeable. Thus when the commons are available, without the kind of relevant and enforceable constraints to action that are erected in other spaces (including organizational spaces), no consensus is likely to be reached on the question of how much of its resources ought to be utilized and for what purposes. Indeed, instability is probably inevitable. The larger the commons, the more unlikely or fragile any rough consensus will be. A single defector can dissolve it.

Contrary to Karl Marx, who proclaimed that "The Human essence is the true collectivity of man,"[9] the human being is always in some measure a unique individual. One's idiosyncratic projects therefore need to be tied to some definite sphere of justified personal authority, an area over which one is sovereign; the decisions one makes do not stand in the way of the similar and overlapping projects of others. But in the commons, an individual will be unable to determine just what is to be used properly for his or her own objectives. How one should lay aside resources for future use or replenish resources already used up are questions that cannot be decided for everyone at the same time. And these irresolvable dilemmas will lead to irresolvable conflicts among people, to the tragedy Hardin spoke of.

If, however, the individual is restricted—for example, by a system of private property rights—to drawing resources from some determinate realm (from which others are excluded), he can have a reasonably clear idea as to how to ration resources properly. *For the*

---

9. Karl Marx, *Selected Writings*, ed. David McLellan (London: Oxford University Press, 1977), "On the Jewish Question," p. 126.

resources are his to ration, his entirely; they are within his sole jurisdiction. He gains the benefits of immediate consumption but also bears the costs of inadequate provision for the future, as well as any dumping of bad side effects on others. Both usage and conservation can be accomplished, then, in line with one's own needs and priorities, priorities that may well be quite correct so far as the individual at hand is concerned but inapplicable to someone else.

In a community where private property rights govern nearly everything that people find useful in pursuit of their diverse and various goals, what can be used to realize those goals is quite clear: anything to which one enjoys a private property right. Thus differing goals can, and therefore are likely to be, coordinated. No such coordination is possible in the commons.

Given Hardin's principle, we can expect that many ambitious business entrepreneurs who take advantage of public resources will seem to be trampling on the welfare of other people even as they are also benefiting many of them. They will certainly be seen by many as imposing large costs on those who are not enjoying the benefits, all for the sake of personal profit. When artists or scholars show such ambition, matters tend to be looked at differently since they appear to strive for something deemed inherently worthwhile, not simply some selfish personal advantage, the scourge of modern morality.[10]

10. The following passage from Adam Smith's *The Wealth of Nations* (New York: Random House, 1937, p. 726) sheds light on this fact: "Ancient moral philosophy proposed to investigate wherein consisted the happiness and perfection of a man, considered not only as an individual, but as the member of a family, or a state, and of the great society of mankind. In that philosophy, the duties of human life were treated of as subservient to the happiness and perfection of human life. But, when moral as well as natural philosophy came to be taught only as subservient to theology, the duties of human life were treated of as chiefly subservient to the happiness of a life to come. In the ancient philosophy, the perfection of virtue was represented as necessarily productive to the person who possessed it, of the most perfect happiness in this life. In the modern philosophy, it was frequently represented as almost always inconsistent with any degree of

The goal of personal profit is one source of the constant complaint about special or vested interest politics. And while the rhetoric focuses mainly on the conflict between such special or vested interests and the public interest, in fact most conflict arises among different vested interests. There are, indeed, very few matters that are genuinely in the public or common interest, not excluding many of the concerns of environmentalists.

The extent of the ensuing confusions is indeterminable. In a system of property rights, how many people would be willing to work hard enough to obtain the very things that the more ambitious people are now making use of? Who knows whether and how many people are benefiting indirectly from what is provided directly for others? Just as there may be positive externalities to extremely expensive ventures like the space program, it may also be the case that when a company produces, say, computer parts for some members of the public and in the process pollutes the air, those who suffer the pollution but do not purchase the product will still receive considerable indirect benefits, such as a more developed technology for hospital equipment, transportation, entertainment, athletics, education, or personal computing.

In the commons it is supposed that everyone has an equal entitlement to what are designated as public resources. Nothing belongs to anyone, yet everything belongs to everyone. So when people make use of things, they use what everyone else also owns. Thus, those who are more ambitious will appear to be rude, unfeeling, and greedy for so aggressively making use of the public resource. If I pollute the air I am depriving others and being selfish;

---

happiness in this life, and heaven was to be earned by penance and mortification, not by the liberal, generous, and spirited conduct of a man. By far the most important of all the different branches of philosophy became in this manner by far the most corrupted."

if I spill oil into the ocean I am violating our—meaning also, of course, your—ocean. Or so it seems.

But is one, in fact, really *taking away what is another's* when one uses public property? If one is doing one's best at getting ahead within a commons, can one be rationally blamed if others lag? By definition, in a commons all are free to use or not use resources and even if desirable, no one can reasonably be forbidden the chance to exploit resources. It would be inconsistent with one agent's devotion to his or her goals to lie back and wait until all the resources have been used up by other agents when "they are all entitled."

So we see that from innocent ambition an acrimonious situation develops. There will always be those who believe they have not received their fair share since they *might have been* able to benefit from something that someone else used. Thus, there will always be complaints against those who are ambitious in a commons. The greater the commons, the greater the opportunity for conflict, resentment, and political battle.

On the other hand, in a system of private property the ambitious will be seen, at least by reasonable persons, as having rightfully obtained more to be used for their goals instead of having taken anything from others. For they are making use of private property that at least in principle can be obtained without intruding upon others, by such consensual means as invention, exploration, inheritance, and purchase. Moreover, a private property system encourages what economists call "full cost pricing" and places serious legal obstacles against such abuses as dumping and polluting waters downstream. This is very difficult to achieve in public realms.

Since one cannot know exactly what unfamiliar others want or where their best interest lies, it would be wiser to leave them to rely on their own resources and ambitions—that is, to have a system of private property rights in place. Within such a system, people can be more responsibly productive, as well as more benevolent and less suspicious of one another. They are much less likely than when working with common resources to regard their fellows as "ripping me off."

It is enlightening to consider the failure of socialistic and other collectivist political arrangements from the perspective of the tragedy of the commons. That any type of large collective organization, especially a coercive one, will "remorselessly generate" this tragedy is not sufficiently appreciated by those who seek to salvage coercive collectivism by giving it a more "human face" in the wake of its dramatic demise in Eastern Europe. Collectivist regimes have certainly suffered environmental spoliation. But as we have seen, there are dimensions of the tragedy of the commons that reach far beyond the problems associated with the environment.

To avoid misunderstanding, none of this counsels against cooperative ventures, brainstorming, teamwork and such. What seems warranted, however, is to make as sure as possible that in all these the participating individual's consent is secured, either implicitly or explicitly. Once that is accomplished, many of the benefits of community actions are uncontestable.

The contributors to this volume all care about sorting out the problems associated with the commons. Some focus on the environment. Others look into related problems such as public finance, collective responsibility (pride or guilt), and democratic decision making or management. What the authors share is a realization that linking actions and consequences to individuals is usually a vital and just social policy for human community life. They examine the difficulties human beings face when they try to solve their problems without the benefit of a system of individual rights, including the right to private property. Their work adds to the growing literature of a new individualist social political analysis that instead of seeing persons as isolated atoms recognizes the vital individuality of everyone and the ways in which social and political institutions can accommodate that individuality.

CHAPTER ONE

Is Bad Conduct Always Wrong?
The Ethics of Environmental Effects

Lester H. Hunt

IN ORDER TO do what I hope to do here, I must begin by trying to elicit and clarify what I believe are some widely held intuitions about a broad class of practical situations. I shall do this by describing and commenting on some examples, and in order to avoid contaminating the reader's response to them, I shall not state, until after some delay, what issue I intend to discuss and what position I shall take in regard to it.

I

The first case should sound familiar to people who work in universities and other bureaucracies. A group of people meet regularly as a committee, to make decisions regarding the place where they work. Because the issues they discuss are important to each of them, each member typically speaks at every meeting in order to place before the group information and arguments that he or she believes

Part of the first draft of this paper was written during a stay at the Center for Study of Public Choice at George Mason University, which was made possible by a generous grant from the Center.

are relevant to those issues. Each of them has additional incentives to speak up, for speaking affords the pleasure of self-expression and the rare joy of hearing a speech that consists entirely of the truth. Because of these additional incentives, each speaks a bit longer than is really necessary to communicate information and arguments effectively. As a result, although no one person speaks for a very long time, the meetings tend to last at least fifteen minutes longer than the two hours officially allowed for each session. All the members find this quite annoying. It happens every time they meet.

What judgments about the behavior of these people do we find it natural to make? One is certainly inclined to say that it would be better if they did not talk so long. It seems likely that the annoyance each feels at the length of the meetings is greater than the pleasure each feels at speaking too long. Suppose that this is true. What does it signify? It seems to mean that they shouldn't behave as they do, that they ought to do something else. But here some care is necessary to avoid exaggerating the force that this "shouldn't" and this "ought" have. Contrast this judgment to the one we would make if a single individual, one great bore, were to produce the same effect that in the present case the members bring about collectively—talking at least fifteen minutes longer than is necessary. Such behavior, we would think, is wrong. In the present case, on the other hand, the notion that they "shouldn't" act this way means that it would be better if they didn't, not that what they do is wrong. In this sense, we recognize no strict moral requirement that they do otherwise. This point becomes perhaps more obvious if we contrast the behavior of the members to that of a single member who makes a point by gratuitously insulting other members of the committee.

In the second case, a group of traders are speculating on the price of tulip bulbs. Though they are mostly unknown to one another, they are participants in a web of behavior in which each responds to signals from the others that are received in the form of changes in the price of the goods they are trading. Their speculation drives the price of the bulbs higher and higher, until most stand to make a significant amount of money from their enterprise. One day, the price of the bulbs dips and continues to fall for a short while. Each participant has the same notion of what this may well mean. There is some likelihood that the price will drop enough to cost one money in the event that one does not sell out soon. On the other hand, each knows that if one does sell out soon, one might be contributing in some measure to a further drop in the price and consequently to the detriment of those who do not sell. Most of them sell out, the price plunges, and the few who are tardy in selling are ruined.

Once again, one would say that things would plainly have been better if these people had done something other than what they did, and it is possible to think (perhaps by straining a bit) that they in fact should have done otherwise. Further, it does not seem possible to think that they have done wrong. This fact can be brought into sharper relief by comparing their behavior with that of a speculator who knowingly causes a panic in the tulip bulb market by making a suitably large sale.

For the third case, suppose there is a town in which, for some reason, only two types of automobile are available. One type, the Whippet, is small and, because it uses relatively little fuel, is relatively nonpolluting. The other type, the Leviathan, is safer for driver and passengers in the event of a collision because it is larger than a Whippet, but for the same reason it uses more fuel and is more polluting. Fuel is very cheap and plentiful and no one is very concerned with conserving it. Anyone contemplating buying a Leviathan knows that they will have to breathe a portion of the extra pollution they produce, but even though the town is situated in a valley that is often covered by a temperature inversion layer that tends to trap air pollution, they know that the amount of pollution they impose on any one person is rather small. Most of the townspeople, having taken all these factors into consideration, own Leviathans. The town is often covered with an annoying and unhealthy layer of smog. For each Leviathan driver, in fact, the effects of the extra smog produced by all the Leviathans are more than enough to cancel out the benefits of driving one.

As before, one wants to say that it would be better if these people were to behave differently by, in this case, driving Whippets instead of Leviathans. It is at least plausible to say that this is what they should do. But, once again, this does not seem to mean that what they are doing is morally wrong—as it would be if one individual (an industrialist, perhaps) were to produce the entire increment of smog singlehandedly for reasons similar to those that move the townspeople to produce it collectively.

In making moral judgments about unwelcome social effects we seem to observe an important distinction between certain cases in which a single individual is responsible for the entire effect and certain others in which responsibility is dispersed over a number of individuals. In some of these cases we also observed another distinction. Both in the case of the loquacious committee and in the case of the polluting drivers, the individual is responsible for an effect that is repeated or continuous over long periods of time. Here we can be seen to discriminate on the basis of how the effect is dispersed across time. For instance, if the committee in the first example has seven members and each meeting lasts fifteen minutes too long, then each member speaks an average of fifteen minutes too long every seven meetings. If a member were to speak fifteen minutes too long at one meeting out of seven we would be strongly inclined to think that the speaker was violating some requirement that applies to members of committees, even if the same person did not speak too long at the other six meetings. Yet the loquacious speaker would not be wasting more time than members we judge in a categorically more lenient manner. We are prepared to discriminate in the same sort of way in the case of the polluting drivers. If there are sixty Leviathan drivers in town, each produces on the average enough pollution every two months to create, under the right conditions, one smoggy day if it were released in one huge gust. Imagine there is an individual who does not drive a Leviathan but does precisely that, for reasons that are no worse than those that move people to drive Leviathans. Perhaps the individual is an industrialist who is saving some money—not very much—on production methods, or perhaps he or she is conducting a sophisticated experiment concerning the effects of eye and sinus irritation on human behavior. This, I am sure we would want to say, is wrong.

Moral philosophers have discussed the possibility that there are actions that, though morally meritorious, are nonetheless not morally required of us. The consensus among most of those who have written on ethical problems seems to be that such actions do exist.[1] We have just encountered an idea that in an obvious way is analogous to this one but is apt to be more controversial among ethical theorists, the idea that there are actions that are bad—bad in terms of consequences which do seem to be morally significant—but not wrong. Whether we want to incorporate this idea into our moral theories or not, it does seem to me a part of our positive morality, the moral principles that determine the pretheoretical judgments that we actually make. My examples indicate that this idea, as it is embedded in ordinary moral judgments, covers a wide range of situations. In some, the relevant consequences are physical effects such as the transmission of particles and gasses from one place to another, in others they lie merely in the way in which the affected parties interpret symbolic or communicative behavior. In some the group of interacting individuals is large and in others it is small; in some they know each other and in others they do not.

---

1. For comments on some contributions to this literature, see Shelly Kagan, "Does Consequentialism Demand Too Much? Recent Work on the Limits of Obligation," *Philosophy and Public Affairs* 13, no. 3 (1984): 239–54.

These situations do seem to resemble one another, however, in the nature of the incentives and costs confronting the agent who produces the relevant consequences. Later on, I shall clarify the idea we have encountered here by explaining the nature of this resemblance. Eventually, I shall try to explain why we have the moral intuitions that we do seem to have about situations of this kind. Finally, I shall briefly suggest reasons for suspecting that positive morality is correct in the position it takes concerning such situations, that perhaps these intuitions are as they should be. First, though, I shall pause to examine some obstacles that stand in the way of this last suggestion. As we shall see, some extremely respectable theories can be used to argue that positive morality, in these cases, is simply wrong.

II

Whatever else one might think of them, the three examples I have described represent social problems, since they are clearly instances of people who, whether they are acting wrongly or not, are certainly doing something that is harmful. The idea that I have identified as part of positive morality is clearly compatible with the notion that, when it is possible, something should be done about these problems. It is compatible, for instance, with the notion that institutions should somehow be designed that alter the relevant incentives and costs in such a way as to eliminate the unwelcome effects that they elicit. There is an extensive literature, written mainly by economists, in which institutional changes of this sort are defended as solutions to the problem of pollution. These solutions are subject to some of the same objections as the thesis I mean to defend and it should shed some light on the problems I am treating here if we examine them briefly.

From the point of view of many economists, the root of the problem of pollution lies in the fact that the normal arrangement of property rights, in which the atmosphere and large bodies of water are in effect treated as a "commons," permits people to use the environment as a free waste sink, imposing much of the cost of waste disposal on other people. This means, among other things, that some of the total cost of producing an economic good does not fall within the scope of the producer's accounting system, and whenever this happens, pollution will be overproduced. There is a level of pollution that would be worth the cost, but as long as people do not have to take account of the entire cost of what they do, human action will not find that level. One policy that has often been proposed by economists as a remedy for pollution resulting from manufacturing is the use of a tax which is variously called a "residuals charge" or an "effluent fee." This policy would impose a per-unit tax on objectionable emissions that would be equivalent to the unaccounted-for, external cost of the emissions. Other taxes might then be reduced by an amount equal to the pollution taxes that are paid. The market would automatically find the level of pollution that is worth the cost, partly by reducing the consumption of goods that can only be produced by methods that cause pollution and partly by shifting production to less polluting fields.

In spite of the widespread support among economists for policies like this one, the pollution-control measures actually adopted in the United States and elsewhere have almost always represented an entirely different approach. The usual policy is one of "direct regulation," in which pollution, or at least certain forms of it, is declared to be a legal offense and subject to punitive measures such as fines. Economists have usually explained this striking divergence between expert opinion and actual practice by appealing to the self-interest of the agents who influence actual practice. Some have pointed out that the system actually in operation enables politicians to shift responsibility for controversial decisions to unelected bureaucrats who, not having to garner votes, can shift the cost of pollution abatement to agents who have little influence over the political system. Others have claimed that, under certain circumstances, the limits that direct regulation places on production actually have beneficial pecuniary effects on manufacturers, the same sorts of effects that cartelization has.[2]

As some of the same authors have pointed out, however, special interests are probably not the only factor that obstructs implementation of the pollution tax policy; there are also "widely accepted ethical norms" that stand in its way.[3] For our purposes, the most important moral objection to this policy is that it merely "sells the right to pollute."[4] As a mere description of the facts, this claim is correct and penetrating: the pollution tax is not a punishment, like a fine, and therefore it does not convey, as part of its expressive function, the conviction that pollution as such is wrong. The pollution tax is simply a price that is meant to express the value of the environment as a waste sink. To constitute an objection, this claim must assume that pollution is wrong. What reason is there to believe this assumption? Unfortunately, it seems to follow quite naturally from any one of three different widely accepted ethical theories. This means that any of these theories can also be used against the thesis I wish to defend in this essay, at least as it applies to pollution and to any social problem that relevantly resembles it.

First, at least one sort of hypothetical contract theory of morals could easily be used to argue that the polluting drivers in my example are doing something morally wrong in driving Leviathans. Such a theory would state something to the effect that people are morally obligated to follow whatever rules it would be in their

2. J. M. Buchanan and G. Tullock, "Polluter's Profits and Political Response: Direct Controls Versus Taxes," *American Economic Review* 65, no. 1 (1975): 139–47.

3. Ibid., p. 143.

4. See Vincent Barry, *Moral Issues in Business* (Belmont, Calif.: Wadsworth, 1983), p. 331.

interest to agree on, supposing that agreements were possible and that everyone's compliance with the rules were somehow guaranteed. Whippet drivers and nondrivers would clearly have an interest in agreeing to a rule prohibiting the use of Leviathans, and Leviathan drivers would as well, since the aggregate undesirable effects of all the Leviathan drivers are greater for them than the differential benefits of driving one of the more-polluting cars. Thus, everyone has good enough reason to agree to a rule prohibiting the use of Leviathans, even if there is no veil of ignorance preventing them from knowing to which section of the population they belong. This would mean that this sort of hypothetical contract theory would imply that driving the more-polluting type of automobile is morally wrong.

The same result would follow if one begins with a utilitarian account of what is morally required. If we make the necessary assumption that the utilities of different individuals can be compared, it is impossible to avoid thinking that, even though the negative effect a Leviathan driver (as compared with a Whippet driver and a nondriver) has on any one individual is small, the sum of these negative effects taken together is greater than the benefits that the driver could only get from driving a Leviathan. In the choice between driving a Leviathan and not driving one, then, the utility of everyone affected is maximized by not driving one. An act-utilitarian moral theory would therefore require one not to drive a Leviathan. The same result would follow from a rule-utilitarian theory.

Utilitarianism and hypothetical contract theories could also be used to show that the members of the loquacious committee are acting wrongly. They could also, with some plausibility, do the same thing for the individuals who sold out and precipitated the tulip bulb panic. A third moral theory, the neo-Lockean natural rights view, is probably more limited in its application, but it seems to have even stronger implications for cases of pollution.[5] In this view, everyone enjoys a morally inviolable domain consisting of one's own person and property, and anyone who invades that domain without permission—at least if it is an invasion that one would prevent if one could—is violating one's rights and therefore is doing something that is morally wrong. One can commit such a wrongful invasion by bringing one's person into the domain of another, as in cases of trespass. One can do so also by initiating a process in which some physical entity enters the domain of another. This would include launching a bullet, hurling a burning torch, and carelessly parking a truck on a hill with its brake off. It would also include doing things that send particles, fluids, gasses, or vibrations into the domain of another person—at least if the person would have prevented their entry if that were possible. This means that wrongful invasion would include all activities that we would normally regard as polluting. Thus, although a neo-Lockean natural rights view may not regard the behavior of the people in my first two cases as morally wrong, because they might not involve invasions of this sort, it would certainly seem to imply that the behavior of the Leviathan drivers, along with all polluting behavior, is morally wrong.

III

In spite of the implications of these influential ethical theories, positive morality contains no rules that imply that the bad conduct in

5. The most familiar current version of this view is to be found in Robert Nozick's *Anarchy, State, and Utopia* (New York: Basic Books, 1974). For a sophisticated and very interesting defense of direct antipollution regulation that is based on neo-Lockean natural rights theory, see Richard A. Epstein, "Nuisance Law: Corrective Justice and Its Utilitarian Constraints," *Journal of Legal Studies* 8 (1979): 49–102. Nozick (pp. 79–81) favors treating pollution as a tort. Such a policy would not differ from direct regulation in a way that is relevant to my present purposes because it, too, involves treating pollution as a legal offense.

the cases I have described is wrong. I shall now try to explain why this is so.

Consider the nature of the situations that such rules would govern. In each situation, there are no psychologically salient rights that the bad conduct would violate, other than the rights that are specified by the rule itself, if it exists. Whether such a rule exists or not, however, the individuals involved have other reasons for acting. They know that they are in a situation in which (1) all have a choice to make and (2) definite results, which in one degree or another are desirable or undesirable, will follow for each of them from the choices that they all make. Situations that have these two characteristics are what game theorists call "games." In the cases I pose, the "players" have two options and the results of the game are related to their options in definite ways. In each case, there is one option that is such that (*a*) if all or most of them do not take it, the results for all are undesirable, (*b*) if all or most of them do take it, the results for all are desirable, while (*c*) for any set of choices on the part of the others, each achieves a better result by not taking it than by taking it, and (*d*) those who do not take it diminish to some extent the desirability of the results obtained by those who do. Rather obviously, this description also fits the familiar Prisoner's Dilemma, and games that have characteristics *a* through *d* have been called "generalized Prisoner's Dilemma structured situations."[6]

6. Edna Ullmann-Margalit, *The Emergence of Norms* (Oxford: Oxford University Press, 1977), pp. 25–27. In case the relationship to the Prisoner's Dilemma is not obvious, consider this typical Prisoner's Dilemma matrix:

	C1:	C2:
R1:	3,3	0,5
R2:	5,0	1,1

Characteristic *a* correctly describes the R2-C2 outcome, and *b* describes the R1-C1 outcome. Applied to this matrix, *c* states that each player gets better results from strategy 2, whatever the other one does, and *d* states that the result for a

In my examples, a rule strictly prohibiting the bad conduct would bring everyone involved into the desirable state of affairs described in *b*. This fact, however, certainly does not distinguish between rules that do not and should not exist and ones that undoubtedly do and should exist. It has been suggested, very plausibly, I think, that all or most of the basic duties of morality resolve situations which have the same four characteristics by bringing everyone involved into a state of affairs that fits the description in *b*.[7] Nonetheless, such duties do differ with regard to the motives one has for following them from the class of rules I am discussing here, and the difference is closely relevant to the point I wish to make. One can see the difference, in fact, precisely by considering some implications of the fact that behavior that conforms to basic moral duties can represent a benign solution to a Prisoner's Dilemma situation. As an example of a basic moral duty, I shall take the familiar idea that one owes aid to those in need. As would be the case with the class of rules I have been discussing here, the behavior that the rule requires is something to which the beneficiary has no salient rights other than those that are specified by the rule itself. But there are certain motives external to the rule that tend to support the behavior that follows it. We can see that this is so if we first note how situations in which people are in need of help can present a Prisoner's Dilemma structure.[8]

Suppose that two men, R and C, regularly have lunch at the same cafeteria. From time to time, one of them finds that he hasn't

---

player who takes 1 when the other takes 2 are worse than would have resulted had the other taken 1 as well.

7. Ibid., p. 38 n. 5. For a classic statement, see David P. Gauthier, "Morality and Advantage," *Philosophical Review* 76, no. 4 (1967): 460–75.

8. The ideas in the following two paragraphs are mainly taken from Robert Axelrod, *The Evolution of Cooperation* (New York: Basic Books, 1984), and from Robert L. Trivers, "The Evolution of Reciprocal Altruism," *Quarterly Review of Biology* 36, no. 1 (1971): 38–39. The example I use is my own.

enough money on him to buy lunch when the other is able to help him out by giving or lending him the needed money. Rendering assistance would cost either of them a definite amount of well-being: two units. But receiving the same assistance when one is in need is worth considerably more than what one loses by helping, and I shall suppose this benefit amounts to six units. The situation becomes a recurring Prisoner's Dilemma if we suppose that R and C alternate in coming up short, with first one and then the other needing help. The first two emergencies and all succeeding pairs are described by the following matrix:

$$
\begin{array}{ccc}
 & \text{C1:} & \text{C2:} \\
\text{R1:} & 4,4 & -2,6 \\
\text{R2:} & 6,-2 & 0,0
\end{array}
$$

Strategy 1 is giving assistance; strategy 2 is not giving assistance. Each occurrence of this Prisoner's Dilemma game places both R and C in one of the cells of the matrix. If both have given (and received) help at the end of one play, both get a result of 4 (= 6 − 2). If neither of them incurs the costs of helping, neither of them will receive the benefits of being helped and both will get 0.

As the off-diagonal cells indicate, this situation makes it possible for one person to gain at another's expense: it is possible to accept help without returning it. But a comparison between the diagonal cells also indicates that it presents the possibility of gains from co-operation: mutual help is at all events better for both parties than mutual indifference. Moreover, it has a characteristic that can promote cooperation, in that it is a situation of mutual power, since the results each party gets depends on what they *both* do.[9] To pro-

9. This point tends to be pushed into the background in discussions of Prisoner's Dilemma situations, many of which treat it as virtually the paradigm of all social evils. See, e.g., Gordon Tullock, *The Social Dilemma* (Blacksburgh, Va.: University Publications, 1974), esp. chap. 1. The relationship between a capitalist and a labor union has Prisoner's Dilemma characteristics that admittedly can cause

mote his own self-interest, each player must care about what the other does, and since this is an iterated game in which each party knows what the other has done, each must care about the other's response to his own behavior. To some extent, each has an interest in accepting help without giving it, since this would guarantee oneself a result of 6 in one occurrence of the game. But this would tend to work against one's interests in future plays, for it would provide the other player with evidence that such unhelpful behavior will continue—a prospect that would mean that it is in his self-interest to "punish" one's unhelpfulness by being unhelpful oneself, since he would thereby expect a result of 0 instead of −2. In the long run, each has a motive to avoid discouraging the other from being helpful, and one can only do this by being helpful oneself. If this motivational feature of the situation is known to both players and known to be sufficiently strong, mutual help will follow.

Thus there is at least one motivational feature of situations in which people are in need that exists independently of a duty to render aid and supports behavior that conforms to it. Viewed in the light in which I have shown it so far, helping behavior presents the appearance of a mere insurance scheme. Of course, this is not the appearance it presents in the world around us, but this should not be surprising. At least sometimes, people in the world around us help each other in part from a sense of duty, and this helps to differentiate such behavior from an insurance scheme. But rules that specify duties are not the only source of actual helping behavior that distinguishes it from a sort of insurance. Human beings have a certain tendency, which is sometimes very strong, to take an interest in the interests of others. It includes trying on occasion to alle-

---

problems, but to understand situations of this sort fully we should compare them with others, such as those between masters and slaves, that lack such characteristics and *for that reason* contain fewer possibilities of cooperation to mutual advantage. A Prisoner's Dilemma is not a situation of exploitation with impunity.

viate the perceived sufferings of others and appears to exist to some extent independently of the requirements of positive morality. Without implying any psychological speculations about the source of this tendency, we can follow Hume and Adam Smith in calling the tendency "sympathy."[10] When a player's turn comes up in the game I have described, he knows that the other player is in need, that he is in a position to relieve that need, and that if he does not do so the need will persist until it is relieved in some other way. This is a motive for taking option 1 which does not appear in the payoff structure, and it obviously can be a powerful motive.

To the extent that the principle that one must render aid to those in need governs conduct in Prisoner's Dilemma situations, the nature of these situations appeals to both self-interest and sympathy in ways that support behavior that conforms to the principle. It is obvious that both factors have an important influence on actual conduct in which people follow this principle and that both of them help to explain why such behavior exists. The same things can be said, with approximately the same force, for most of the other principles that specify the basic duties of positive morality, including the rules that require truth-telling and promise-keeping, and the ones that forbid theft and aggressive violence.

The same things, however, could not be said of the rules that would forbid the bad conduct that occurred in the three situations I cited at the outset. These situations did not appeal either to self-interest or to sympathy in ways that would support such rules. This is because, unlike the game of helping, these situations are ones not of mutual power but of mutual powerlessness. This in turn is in large part due to the fact that while the helping game is a two-person game, these situations affect the individuals involved as N-

---

10. By assembling a number of ingenious examples, Smith argues persuasively that sympathy is such a primitive human response that it must not depend on morality for its existence. See *The Theory of Moral Sentiments* (Oxford: Oxford University Press, 1979), I; sect. 1, chap. 1.

person games. A player is someone who both receives payoffs and determines the payoffs of any one occurrence of the same game jointly with the other players, so that the results of an occurrence of a two-person game are determined by two agents and those of an N-person game by more than two.

It is widely recognized that the difference between these two types of game can have very important consequences. In my three troublesome cases, the power of each player is such that the effect that any one player has on any other is not significant, in that neither the agent nor the patient clearly perceives it as affecting the patient's well-being: the effects produced by any one player are diffused among all the other players. But the aggregate effect produced by all the players for any one player is significant. This further limits each player's exercise of power in several important ways. In the helping game, each player has two possible moves, and it was crucial to the way in which self-interest led to mutual aid that: (1) each player had a self-interested motive for making the move that is less beneficial to the other player if that is what the other does, and (2) doing so is perceptibly damaging to the other player. In the three N-person situations both these conditions are entirely absent: none can make a move that is perceptibly damaging to any one player because none has any significant effects on any one player at all. And the (insignificant) effects one does have fall on all the others regardless of how they play. Further, no one has a motive to invent some way to damage those who make the less beneficial choice because no one feels that any one person is harming or failing to benefit them in a significant way. In addition—again, because no one has significant effects on any one person—the situation does not appeal to sympathy as a motive for mutually beneficial behavior. There are no salient damaging effects with which to sympathize. In general, the promptings of self-interest are entirely on the side of making the less socially beneficial move oneself and do nothing to motivate one to impel others to do anything else, whereas sympathy is unable to compensate for this insufficiency of self-interested considerations.

There is an easy way to describe this sort of N-person situation more generally and more clearly. The person who makes the more beneficial choice is providing a good that is scarce (in the sense that everyone would prefer to have more of it at a low enough cost) and costs the individual something to produce. The fact that this good is "diffused" across the other players of the game means that, in addition to its scarcity and costliness, it has the other characteristics of what economists call a "public good": (1) once it is provided for someone, the additional cost of providing it for someone else is zero, and (2) there is no way to exclude anyone from receiving it. In each of the three cases I discussed at the outset, the benefit produced by the more beneficial action is a public good. Other examples of public goods production are refraining from dropping litter in a public place, refraining from contributing to traffic congestion by not driving during rush hour, and refraining from running toward the exit when someone yells "Fire!" in a crowded theater.

If there is an amount of some public good which is such that, if it is produced by enough people the benefits therefrom will exceed the costs for everyone concerned although one's own share of the good that one produces is less than the cost one incurs in producing it, the resulting situation will have characteristics *a* through *d* of the generalized Prisoner's Dilemma structured situation.[11] It will also be a situation in which one cannot encourage production of the

---

11. From the fact that everyone is made better off if the good is produced by a large enough number of those who can do so without their costs exceeding their benefits, characteristics *a* and *b* immediately follow. From the fact that the individual's share of his or her own product exceeds the cost of producing it, it follows that one is always better off not producing it and merely consuming the amount of the good (if any) that is produced by others, and this gives characteristic *c*. This would leave those (if any) who do produce it worse off, and this is *d*.

beneficial results involved by denying them to those who fail to produce—as was done in the helping game—because there is no way to exclude only nonproducers. If, in addition, the share of the good that any person supplies to any one person is not significant, then no one has a motive to punish nonproducers in some other way, and for the same reason no one will be motivated to provide it by considerations of sympathy. This means that situations in which individuals have an opportunity to produce some public good, where the amount of the good that any individual can provide to any one individual is insignificant, differ in an obviously crucial way from a generalized Prisoner's Dilemma situation of the sort modeled in the helping game. In the production of public goods that are diffused in this way, a rule requiring people to do the benign actions described in *b* (in these cases, producing the good) is left unsupported by the incentives that in the other cases are provided by the situation itself.

Behavior that produces such diffused public goods is not the sort of behavior we have learned to expect from others, but it is, at any rate, a far less reliable feature of our social world than behavior that conforms to the basic duties of positive morality. I submit that what we have seen here must be part of the reason why this is so. Compliance with the basic duties of positive morality is relatively reliable and predictable because of the incentives that are built into the situations the rules govern: since compliance is clearly beneficial to some individual or other, it is supported by the promptings of sympathy. In addition, the individuals who could thus be benefited have a motive to punish noncompliance, and they can do so by means of the easy and natural method of denying to those who fail to comply the benefits of their own compliance.

These explanations of some familiar features of human behavior also suggest explanations of certain facts about human beliefs: namely, the intuitions I have been assuming we have concerning the three examples with which I began this essay. In each case we fail to judge that people are acting wrongly when they refrain from producing public goods of the diffused type I have just been describing, and we do so in spite of the fact that everyone who is able to produce the good would be better off if they all did so. The most obviously and directly relevant explanatory factor in this context is that each person's failure to produce the relevant good does no salient damage to anyone, so that the promptings of sympathy provide no motive for producing it. Our ability to sympathize with the harm our actions cause for others provides us with a reason to believe that such actions are wrong, as well as a reason for not doing them. These reasons for thinking an action is wrong are entirely lacking when we refrain from producing public goods like the ones in my three examples, and this lack seems to be a significant one.

It seems to be very difficult for us to see an action as wrong, merely on the basis of its being harmful, if it is not clearly harmful to any specific individual.

The fact that there can be relatively little punishment for failure to produce public goods of this kind also suggests some explanations for our intuitions about such failures, though their explanatory relevance is, I think, less direct than is the case with the insufficiency of sympathy. By itself, the relatively remote chances of being punished simply mean that, so to speak, the cost of cooperative behavior is relatively high: the cost of producing the good is not offset by the thought that by cooperating one has avoided a relatively likely penalty for not producing it. I do not think that this by itself can explain why we do not believe that there is some moral requirement to the effect that we must produce it. Of course, there are some people who possess and effectively use a certain all-too-human ability to make themselves believe that they are not morally required to do whatever would be expensive or inconvenient, but there is no reason to think that this cognitive skill is sufficiently widespread to explain phenomena as nearly universal as the ones we are considering here.

Nonetheless, the high cost of cooperating (if one wants to put it that way) does seem to be part of the reason why people in fact do not cooperate very consistently in contexts like the present one, and this in turn can explain why we tend not to believe that we are obligated to cooperate in such situations. For instance, if people are generally not very reliable when it comes to refraining from littering already littered streets or refraining from speaking a bit too long at meetings, then, unless I am obviously different in this respect, no one will expect me to behave in these ways. This means that they will not come to depend on me to do such things, and consequently will not be disappointed if I should fail to do them. Further, since these same people are unlikely to do such things very consistently themselves, they are unlikely to feel that I am taking advantage of their good behavior without contributing something to them in return. This would seem to mean that though they might believe—as we very often do believe—that such good behavior is just the sort of thing that we ideally ought to be doing, they will probably lack a strongly personal, emotionally charged motive to reproach me for my less than ideal behavior. They will be unlikely to feel that I have disappointed them and exploited their good nature. This means that, though my behavior is actually harmful to other people, I will not expect that whatever advice I might get from them to the effect that I should change my ways will have that peculiar biting or stinging quality that characterizes the reproach we direct at people who violate strict duties toward others.

Furthermore, if I do not observe that such ideal conduct forms anything like a consistent pattern in the world around me, then all the things I have just said of other people will also be true of me. I will not depend on them to behave that way, nor will I be disappointed if they do not, nor will I feel that they are taking unfair advantage of me. I will therefore have no motive to reproach them for their behavior. This, of course, is quite different from the way I would view the behavior of others when they violate strict duties toward other people.

These facts all indicate in various ways that a belief to the effect that we are obligated to behave ideally in these contexts cannot rest on the same sort of social and psychological support that sustains those strict duties toward others that actually are part of our positive morality. The fact that the behavior of the people around me displays a relatively consistent pattern of refraining from robbing and cheating one another, for instance, makes it quite obvious to me that I would face their angry reproaches if I were to break out of this pattern and rob and cheat myself. This salient and enduring possibility of bitterness and blame serves as a very strong reminder to me that—as I believe to be the case—one really should not do such things. It makes my belief so much the more difficult to forget, ignore, or rationalize away. The same is true of the fact that I am disappointed and aggrieved when others violate this pattern of behavior.

The enduring possibility of my own bitterness and blame gives to this belief a psychological presence well beyond what is normally possessed by the more remote and refined ideals. Perhaps most important, the mere presence of the pattern of behavior itself in the world around me serves as a powerful reminder that this is how one should act: it is compelling evidence that others believe that this is how things should be and that they are willing to act on this belief. All these facts serve to explain why the strict duties toward others that are part of positive morality enjoy the widespread and stable acceptance as guides for conduct which in fact they do have. The social context in which we come to believe them also reinforces that belief by making them unforgettable and, psychologically, difficult to evade.

This in turn would explain why we tend not to believe that we have similar duties to produce public goods of the sort I have been discussing. Such beliefs would have to survive without the support that the social context gives to the duties that are actually in force: the explanation would be that they are apparently not able to survive without such support.

IV

This completes my explanation of the intuitions I attempted to elicit in the reader at the outset. I have also claimed that this explanation suggests why there *should* be no rules that run counter to these intuitions. Obviously, no one has to believe this further claim without additional argument to back it up. If an act-utilitarian were to agree to my explanation, he or she might just say that I have merely pointed out a flaw in human nature itself. I have focused on a subset of a certain type of situation—namely, ones in which there are no salient rights involved—in which people normally do make decisions on the basis of utility. This is just what we should always do, according to the act-utilitarian. The flaw lies in the fact that, as I have indicated, we do not—at least not always—make decisions on the basis of utility by summing the utilities of different people. According to the act-utilitarian, if the social benefits of an action exceed their costs, that act should be done, even if no significant benefit falls on any one individual and even if the costs are focused on the one who provides the benefits. This is not a way in which we naturally think—no doubt in part related to the fact, which I referred to early on, that in evaluating the utility effects of one individual we do not do so by summing those effects across time. We can fail to think that it is wrong of a committee member to speak slightly too long in each of seven meetings even though we would think it decidedly wrong to waste the same amount of time in one speech. Sometimes we evaluate the utility effects of actions upon persons one at a time—one act at a time and one person at a time. The act-utilitarian would say that at least part of this is a mistake: we ought to sum the utilities of individuals and do what is most socially beneficial on balance, and such judgment ought to be part of ordinary morality. It should not matter that, if I break the relevant rule, there are not salient injuries with which to sympathize. We should accept the rule in spite of that fact, and in spite of the fact that other people typically do not seem to be willing to follow the rule, and in spite of the fact that neither they nor I will experience strong emotions if someone violates it. More generally, any of the moral theories that are widely accepted could be used to say that it is at least sometimes wrong to fail to provide the sorts of public goods I have described, and, accordingly, they would also imply that facts like these should not be insuperable obstacles in the way of believing the relevant rules. If human nature stands in the way, then human nature is faulty.

Ordinarily, it is easy to say something like "Well, people ought to believe this, and if they don't, they're just wrong." In the present case, though, I don't think it should come quite so naturally. After all, if we accept my explanation, the obstacles that stand in the way of accepting these rules are different in kind from those that usually prevent the masses of human beings from believing the insights of enlightened minorities. It is not that people are being led astray by incorrect ideas, or by the mindless pressure of tradition, or by mere emotional prejudice. The obstacles seem to be less meliorable than that. Because of the insufficiency of natural sympathy in these situations, people are not able to see, vividly, the *point* of the onerous behavior the rules enjoin. The social context in which the rules are to be learned and applied does not naturally lend its influence, as it does in other cases, to making them memorable and impressive enough to form a permanent part of the stock of ideas that are readily available for planning our everyday lives. Given this, the claim that people should believe them anyway seems a hopeless one: it could be that most people never will believe, or not consistently.

Of course, it is still possible to have hope here if one has enough confidence in the influence that ideas and theories have over human behavior. One can still think that we should exert more ideological pressure on those who do not consistently accept these rules. For many centuries human beings have looked to moral leaders and their ideas for guidance, which, in fact, does indeed sometimes win out over supposedly intransigent human nature. Isn't it possible that such methods would work in this case?

The only honest answer I can give to this question is that, although I have given reason to be pessimistic, I cannot deny that such a thing is possible. In that case, one might well ask, why not persist in resisting the intuitions with which I began this essay? If all available ethical theory agrees that at least some of these rules are right, it is surely not foolish to persist if there is a real chance that most people will be converted in their hearts to the true faith at last. My reply to this is that the explanations of human behavior that I have offered here suggest a theoretical reason why such persistence might actually be wrong.

The explanations I have given suggest that to rely on moral leadership in this way and in this context would represent a more profound departure from the way things presently are than one would think. As I have depicted it here, the part of positive morality that consists of strict duties toward others is not a collection of abstract ideas that people learn from moral leaders and then apply to their own conduct. It is a social phenomenon of a very particular sort: insofar as it is a collection of ideas at all, these ideas are rooted in patterns of behavior in which people's interests are related in such a way that the pattern is self-maintaining. Although the rules of positive morality require people to do things that are in the interests of others, people are normally able to adhere to them without sacrifice, since their own compliance is normally in their long-run self-interest. The system of incentives that guarantees that this is so also makes these rules memorable and impressive, so that they are experienced not as abstractions but as everyday realities.

We should expect these facts greatly to enhance the stability of the rules and the pattern of behavior in which they are rooted. Given that our continuing to survive together in peace depends on these rules, their stability is a virtue of great importance. Rules that are only in force because of the influence exercised by moral leaders, and because of our conscientious and deliberate efforts to apply their ideas, are radically different in kind and will inevitably have much less of this important virtue.

Perhaps the rules that are rooted solely in the influence of moral leaders do not belong in the part of positive morality that consists of strict duties toward others. Abstractions and their originators obviously have powerful virtues of their own, but they are also extremely unpredictable. What I should like to suggest—and at this time I only know enough to offer it as a suggestion—is that the rules for which they are the sole basis should be reserved for problems that clearly require their powerful virtues and do not require extremely stable and predictable results.

CHAPTER TWO

Sidestepping the Tragedy of the Commons

Randall R. Dipert

POLITICAL PHILOSOPHY, far more than other branches of philosophy, has invented paradoxes, puzzles, problems, and other devices in order to pose or solve its difficulties. These devices include the Social Contract, the Fable of the Bees, Malthus's problem, the Veil of Ignorance, Arrow's Theorem, and the Prisoner's Dilemma, to name just a few. Contemporary political philosophy has thrived, and careers have been made, from the concoction of supposedly telling lifeboat survival cases, expensive Italian sports cars rolling down the street toward children, and so on. We forget the wise maxim that tricky cases make bad law, and its corollary, that unlikely and artificial situations make bad ethical and political philosophy. It is into this tradition of devices and scenarios—sometimes instructive, sometimes not—that Garrett Hardin's "The Tragedy of the Commons" fits. Exactly why political philosophy has been prone to these methods of analysis is a question I shall eventually attempt to answer.

HEURISTIC DEVICES IN POLITICAL PHILOSOPHY

A quick review of various features of these heuristic methods will be helpful in understanding my later discussion. The Social Contract is a twist on what we could call the "Implicit Contract" that Plato puts into Socrates' mouth as he is on "death row" (*Crito* 50b ff): that by living in Athens, Socrates agreed to abide by its laws and justice, even if those laws later turned against him. He cannot protest his own death sentence too much, or evade it, for that is to undermine the state and to break his implicit promise with the state. The Social Contract, used by Hobbes, Locke, Rousseau, and others, invokes the similar idea of a contract or promise, though its exact status and import are more complex and subtle. The Social Contract claims, first, that there is a *hypothetical* contract that any rational person *would* make, namely, that the protection and defense of rights are ceded to the state. Second, it claims that this hypothetical fact in turn binds us to certain moral obligations to the state. What we would do, if we were rational, legitimizes (some) actual governments for us now.

Although quite appealing, and indeed pragmatically justified by the fine constitutional democracies they have produced, both the Implicit and the Social Contracts have numerous difficulties. One of these (pointed out to me by Tibor Machan) is that both presume a more basic ethical obligation to keep promises—perhaps to keep promises unconditionally. There are further problems: Would all rational people agree to the same things? Is it perfectly clear what rationality *is*, and what rational people would do in all situations? What exactly am I agreeing to with the Implicit or Social Contract? To anything the State, any state at all, wants me to do—Hobbes's notorious sovereign? Without careful, thoughtful, definitive, and widely agreed upon answers to these questions, there is reason to suspect that the Social Contract is more a motivational or pedagogical device than a serious logical argument.[1]

The Veil of Ignorance is Rawls's similarly famous, and famously troubled, device that shows us what political framework a hypothetically rational person *would* agree to if deprived of knowledge concerning that person's real or future assets and abilities, and actual position in a society: such rational people would, Rawls argues, be cautious in consenting to extremely inegalitarian arrangements, or arrangements that deprive minorities of (certain) civil rights, since they might find themselves, once the "veil" is lifted, in one of these unpleasant situations. As has been noted and criticized, the Veil is a very expansive use of hypotheticals, and of rationality itself: it generates more detailed conclusions than the Social Contract, but also seems to require more outright speculation. I can see some empirical basis in the Social Contract, for example: I think most people (never mind about their rationality) would indeed agree to *some* government. I am not sure that most people would even understand the hypothetical condition of the Veil of Ignorance, and I believe that intellectually responsible people would—and should— hesitate to say what they would agree to if they were in that complex and somewhat unbelievable circumstance that the Veil asks us to imagine.

1. We find ourselves agreeing with others' conclusions, but not their premises or arguments. It is as if we *want* to believe that governments, especially democratic governments, are morally justified by some sound logical arguments, and that we all basically appreciate the same arguments. We wink at each other when we notice the gaps in logic or detect the very few premises on which we agree, such as what exactly human nature is. I believe that intellectual integrity requires us to acknowledge the shaky soil in which our most cherished, and widely shared, political beliefs rest. The fact that people I intellectually and morally respect disagree about fundamental assumptions in political theory is itself strong evidence, stronger perhaps than my own intuitions and arguments, about the real epistemological status of these assumptions. I do not *know* them to be true.

The Prisoner's Dilemma is an extremely well-known puzzle in academic political science, economics, and philosophy, but it is not usually an undergraduate topic and it is rarely mentioned in popular discussions of politics. Originating in game theory, it is nevertheless held by many to be a remarkably precise formulation of the most serious impasses that underlie political philosophy. The Tragedy of the Commons has occasionally been regarded as merely a species of the Prisoner's Dilemma. Without going into a full and technical examination, I shall both agree and disagree with this assessment.

The original and simple example of the Prisoner's Dilemma has this format:[2] Two prisoners who have in fact committed a crime together are being held for interrogation. They are being interrogated separately, and each is on his own. If neither confesses, they may either not be convicted or can possibly plead guilty to a much less serious crime—we assume the authorities lack extensive and convincing evidence. If one confesses and the other does not, then the confessing prisoner will receive a much-reduced sentence while the accused nonconfessing prisoner receives the maximum. If both confess, then the authorities are free to sentence both fairly harshly, since they do not require the confession of the other prisoner for conviction.

On the one hand there is some pressure to confess, since neither one knows what the other is doing, and this is the way to avoid the worst punishment. But if both parties behave "rationally" and confess they will both get fairly harsh sentences. It seems that their individual and separate rationality will guide them to a disadvantageous course of action.

There are various ways of describing the predicament. One could say that their separate applications of rationality lead them to

---

2. For an extremely fine discussion of the Prisoner's Dilemma in many of its variants, and with references to the extensive literature, see Steven T. Kuhn's article in the *Stanford* (Internet) *Encyclopedia of Philosophy*, updated April 18, 2000, at http://plato.stanford.edu/entries/prisoner~dilemma.

decisions that are not ideal—perhaps not even rational from an outsider's perspective. One could also say: if only they would co-operate and trust each other, or if only an outside third party (such as a shared defense attorney) would impose a solution, then this would be to their mutual advantage. Here too there is a kind of tragedy: a failure to cooperate.

The Prisoner's Dilemma has the great advantage that, within the mathematical subdiscipline of Game Theory, the situation can be described very exactly and notions of rationality made far more precise than one would have guessed. Roughly, one posits that the value of both confessing is, say, -3 for each. (I use the negative number to estimate the average expected number of years a pris-oner *loses* in prison; in utilitarian terms, the negative value signals pain rather than pleasure.) The value of one confessing and the other not is terrible for the accused, say -4, but not so bad for his accuser, say -1. The value of both stonewalling and not confessing is, say, -2 for each. A payoff matrix, with the various decisions—confess or stonewall—for each prisoner looks like this:

PRISONER B

	Confesses	Stonewalls
Confesses	A:-3/B:-3	$-1/-4$

PRISONER A

Stonewalls	$-4/-1$	$-2/-2$

The exact scheme of numbers for these penalties and benefits is not so important: just so they have roughly the structure above.[3] There

3. More precisely, the values for confessor and accused in the mixed case where one confesses (w) and one doesn't (z) are the extreme values, best and worst values respectively. The value for each when both stonewall is just slightly worse than the value of confessing in the mixed case (x). But the values for both confessing is worse than this (y)—but not as bad as getting accused in the mixed

are some strong background conditions. For one thing, neither prisoner has any idea what the other will do. He can't assign meaningful probabilities to what the other can be expected to do; for all intents and purposes, they are 50 percent that the other prisoner will confess, and 50 percent that he will stonewall.

It is easy to see how each prisoner's reasoning will go. Each prisoner will want to avoid getting stuck with four years in prison—this is a so-called maxi-min strategy that limits the worst case. To avoid the worst case, each will reason that he must confess. But this is worse for each than both stonewalling, though not the very worst case. Also, viewed from the total amount of unhappiness for both parties, the "rational" scenario is the most unhappy one: six years, total, in prison.[4]

Two theoretical extensions of the Prisoner's Dilemma have been studied extensively. One is the *iterated* Prisoner's Dilemma. Here, one tries to determine what strategy, or pattern, of decisions would optimize a player's total winnings if the dilemma were faced over and over again—perhaps by signaling to each other by one's choices or punishing the other party for not cooperating. (It is hard to imagine a truly realistic scenario involving the same two prisoners' getting caught and interrogated repeatedly.) The other is the *multi-player* Prisoner's Dilemma: one considers more than two

---

case. In other words, all that is required for the payoff matrix is that: $w > x > y > z$.

4. One might hesitate over the values I have assigned, since, for example, one might simply want to avoid any prison sentence, or believe that 4 years in prison is not that much worse than 3 (the diminishing marginal negative utility of very bad things). One can exacerbate the paradoxical character by increasing the worst cases (now 4 years in prison) and shaving the next worse case (3 years in prison) so that it is closer to the next best option (now 2 years in prison) but still worse than it. The respective values might then be -10, -3.1, -3 years, and 0. What is still so peculiar is that one will find oneself rationally persuaded to act so that one receives 3.1 years in prison rather than exactly 3.

"prisoners," perhaps even a whole community, each member acting rationally but selfishly.

GARRETT HARDIN'S TRAGEDY OF THE COMMONS

Garrett Hardin's Tragedy of the Commons is intended to be an understandable and gripping problem, and one that seems applicable to a wide variety of real problems—especially environmental ones, as well as to contemporary dilemmas of consumption and overpopulation. It is a more refined puzzle for political philosophy than Malthus's messianic message and it is not patently a hypothetical scenario. Rather, it is a scenario that is intended to be realistic, even historical, and closely to resemble various actual political dilemmas.[5] Likewise, Hardin and many of his commentators have become increasingly—not less—sophisticated in describing the exact nature of the puzzle and have issued proposals to correct the problem it poses with a certain measured zeal. Hardin himself credited the argument to William Forster Lloyd (1794–1852), an Oxford professor of mathematics and economics, in his *Two Lectures on the Checks to Population* (1833). It is also clear that Hardin was influenced by Malthus, since Hardin is most concerned with population control.

Hardin's original formulation is framed in terms of the rationality of the agents and a more or less utilitarian assessment of the overall good. Each herdsman asks him or herself, "What is the utility *to me* of adding one more animal to my herd?" Since the pasture provided by the village Commons is free, and each additional animal can be obtained at a cost that, together with labor and minor supply

---

5. For evidence that there was no real, historical problem of the commons in England, see Susan Cox and Jane Buck, "No Tragedy of the Commons," *Environmental Ethics* 1985, no. 7: 49–72. This supports my view that, over time, constraints on exploitation will naturally evolve, either as a matter of law or as a culturally enforced "understanding."

costs, is well below what the animal can later be sold for, it is clear that—up to a very large number—it is rational for the herdsman to add an animal. (Or so it *seems*: I don't actually believe that this is what is most rational in truly realistic settings.)

This reasoning is, of course, duplicated by other herdsman, and the result is a ravaging of the Commons, eventually making all the herdsmen far worse off than they would be with relatively small herds that used the Commons sparingly or not at all. Hardin is less concerned with the aesthetic and possibly intrinsic damage done to nature than are many contemporary environmentalists. His concern is the expected long-term impact on aggregate humankind. The tragedy for Hardin is thus not (especially) the environmental one, but a human tragedy:

> Each man is locked into a system that compels him to increase his herd without limit—in a world that is limited. Ruin is the destination toward which all men rush, each pursuing his own best interest in a society that believes in the freedom of the commons. Freedom in a commons brings ruin to all.[6]

As a later brief commentary (1993) on this original quotation, Hardin notes that the tragedy results from "commonized herds + privatized herds."[7] (The original quotation seems to be criticizing "freedom" itself, but in the unrestricted sense in which people attempt to justify doing anything they want by saying it's a "free country.") His later emphasis seems to be on the instability of a *mixed* system: we could obtain stability either by having both herds and commons made public (either publicly managed or un-owned—perhaps communal), or by privatizing both. His logic and

6. Garrett Hardin, "The Tragedy of the Commons," *Science*, December 13, 1968, pp. 1243–48.

7. Garrett Hardin, *Living within Limits* (New York: Oxford University Press, 1993), pp. 216–18. See also Garrett Hardin, "Second Thoughts on 'The Tragedy of the Commons,'" in Herman E. Daly, ed., *Economics, Ecology, Ethics: Essays Toward a Steady-State Economy* (San Francisco: W. H. Freeman, 1973).

this gloss permits *either* possibility of escape from the dilemma. The problem of exploitation and ruin occurs when one is privatized and the other is not.

In his later retelling of the Tragedy, Hardin rushes in to correct those who are simplistically anti-greed from endorsing his position as their own:

> . . . the destruction of an overpastured common is likely to be blamed on the greed of individual herdsmen. *Blaming misses the point.* Each human being, like every other animal, is genetically programmed to seek his own good. "Prudence is," as Lloyd said, "a selfish virtue"—and, since prudence makes for survival, natural selection justifies the word *virtue*.[8]

It is clear that for Hardin, the tragedy consists of individuals pursuing what is rational for each, only to have their separate and collective well-being greatly diminished by the fact of everyone's pursuing this "rational" strategy. Individualized rationality does not produce overall maximization, hence it is not (from this overall, global perspective) rational.

Expressed in this way, the Tragedy of the Commons appears to be just an instance of the Prisoner's Dilemma, and suggests either the rationality of internal "cooperation" among the herdsmen, external "regulation," or privatization of the once-public good.

What precisely corresponds to a "commons"? In other words, to what phenomena is the Tragedy of the Commons supposed to apply by analogy? Natural resources come most often to mind. But since food and land are already largely privatized, the best examples seem to be air, water, and oceans beyond territorial limits (as well as things in them, such as fish).

Some have suggested that the Internet—or information itself—

---

8. Hardin, *Living within Limits*, p. 218.

is a commons, and will become "overgrazed."[9] Although increasing need for bandwidth on the Internet by intensive purposes such as video, pictures, and live audio are examples of such phenomena, it is a widespread misconception that the increasing number of users leads to slowdowns in the World Wide Web. There is economic pressure on Internet service providers to supply increased response, access, and computing power, and since these servers are themselves nodes in the WWW, capacity is thereby automatically increased. Servers are simultaneously access points and information conduits. It is as if the intensive grazing by more cattle just caused the grass to grow faster by an amount that magically matched demand.

It has proven all too easy to see a "Tragedy" of the "Commons" in many phenomena.

THE THIRD WAY OUT OF THE ALLEGED TRAGEDY

Political philosophers considering the Tragedy of the Commons have generally seen only two solutions. They think the choice for resolving the Tragedy (and the instability between what is individually rational and overall rational) is between regulating the Commons or privatizing the Commons. Those on the Left have tended to promote the course of regulating the Commons; this typically amounts to state ownership.[10] This solution amounts to solving the problem of mixed public-private clash by making everything public. The herds are not completely "nationalized," of course, but

9. See C. M. Rosen and G. M. Carr, "Fares and Free Riders on the Information Highway," *Journal of Business Ethics* 16 (1997): 1439–45.

10. For this view, which I think is quite misguided, see John Roemer, "A Public Ownership Resolution of the Tragedy of the Commons," *Social and Political Philosophy* 1989, no. 6: 57–71. This is actually what I would call a "pseudo-public" arrangement. A more theoretically pure—but wildly unrealistic—solution would be to leave all resources unowned or communal.

restrictions are placed on what they may do: they may not feed unrestrictedly at the Commons, although it is "public." Equivalently, one might see the Commons as privatized, but under the ownership of an entity called The State. Though ownership by this legal fiction preserves the façade that the land is still "public," it can no longer be used by anyone who wishes to do so, and access is controlled by some codified procedure.

Those on the Right have likewise tended to level or equalize the mixed private-public condition that gives rise to the dilemma. They propose privatizing the once unowned or "public" entity and allocating it to real people, not a legal fiction such as The State.[11] This argument is more fragile than is often thought, however, and is ultimately dependent on arguments from efficiency, and not arguments from justice and rights.

What is ignored, I think, is a "Third Way" that becomes apparent only when one realizes that the Tragedy of the Commons is a particular example of the Prisoner's Dilemma. One also has to think of the Prisoner's Dilemma in a certain way, with special attention to far more realistic scenarios than is usual. The third way consists in the possibility that the herdsmen themselves will begin to *cooperate*, either in advance of the ruination of the Commons because they are rational and thoughtful and thus recognize the danger, or because they have experienced its destruction or similar "tragedies" before. This cooperation will consist of agreements that they them-

---

11. For this position, see Randy E. Barnett, "Contract Remedies and Inalienable Rights," *Social and Political Philosophy* 1986, no. 4: 179–202. Barnett argues that crime is a "commons" problem—a bit of a stretch, although it is easy to see (graffiti, soliciting, harassing) that some crimes are exacerbated by public property (commons). Yet there is no rational tendency for all of us to abuse this space or resource, which is surely a condition for reasonably calling it a "commons" problem. The word "commons" and its manifold tragedies have become a buzzword applied to all manner of things. See, e.g., Robert Solomon's criticism of Ed Hartman's claim that a corporation is a commons in "The Corporation as Community: A Reply to Ed Hartman," *Business Ethics Quarterly* 1994, no. 4: 271–85.

selves initiate, either implicitly or explicitly. Strategies for punishing violators of this accord will also arise spontaneously. The rational strategy for the joint use of the Commons that will emerge bears a close resemblance to the "saddle points" that emerge in the iterated Prisoner's Dilemma. Though the benefits for any particular individual are not maximal under this scenario—for that would consist in unlimited exploitation by that individual alone—they are optimal in the sense that they are "the best that can be (rationally) hoped for," given the possibility of cooperation among rational, autonomous agents, and especially among those who regard themselves as in some important sense "equal" or "like" the other agents. One might think of this option as the formation of voluntary arrangements outside of the usual notion of property and ownership, and accompanying rights.

If individuals learn to cooperate from an actual past incident of overuse, another way of portraying this version is to say that maybe the Tragedy of the Commons is most often no tragedy at all. It is a temporary difficulty, and a learning experience, which will induce rational cooperation so that forms of it are then frequently avoided by truly rational agents who learn.

It is peculiar that Hardin and many other commentators have not seen the similarity to the Prisoner's Dilemma (particularly when Hardin was writing after the Prisoner's Dilemma became well known as a touchstone of political philosophy). I would conjecture that Hardin does not conceptualize the matter more broadly because he is hostage to various strong claims concerning biological determinism. We can see this from the language he uses: "Each [herdsman] is locked into a system that compels him" (1968) and "Each human being, like every other animal, is genetically programmed to seek his own good" (1993). In this latter quotation, Hardin is apparently assuming that each herdsman is thinking blindly and "atomistically," and will not see any predicament before it arises, will not learn from past experiences, and will not cooperate "for his own good." In other words, he does not see any role for rationality, deliberation, and for the ability of individual creatures—even nonhumans—to grasp and react to the Tragedy as a contemplated and often-encountered scenario. Because he does not see the agents as able to choose, as able to play a "game," there is for him no "dilemma," only tragedy. This is ultimately quite puzzling from a logical point of view, since by publishing the Tragedy he clearly wants to influence people to avoid it, which we cannot do if we are all blindly driven by biological "programming."

THE TRAGEDY OF THE COMMONS AND
A REALISTIC PRISONER'S DILEMMA

I think the Prisoner's Dilemma is quite artificial and distant from the everyday situations human beings encounter (at least as the Dilemma is ordinarily described). Nevertheless, I believe it exhibits quite well certain key features of the real experiences that give rise to our deepest political problems. The extreme artificiality of the simple Prisoner's Dilemma can be exposed rather quickly. I am rarely in such a position with *just one* other competitor, with *no* knowledge of the other's probable decision, and with all known benefits hinging on a single decision between only two choices, and that arises just once. Instead, encountering such a situation for real and in the wild, so to speak, it is likely we would reason that the other prisoner is just as rational as I am; consequently, if I see the dilemma in advance, then the other prisoner will too. I can further guess that he will guess that I will see it, etc. Furthermore, our social life consists of a very large number or sequence of transactions, involving all kinds of exchanges of everything from a "good morning," a kiss, letting a pedestrian cross the street, to risking one's life to save another. The negative exchanges involve everything from a frown of disapproval, an uncomplimentary remark, to a conspiracy to destroy a career. Life does not consist of just one, isolated, critical transaction on just one occasion, and does not occur outside of a system of language, custom, and (known) history of social transactions by people like you and me. We play a vast and overlapping number of "games" with punishments and rewards—and applications of tit-for-tat—being *cross-modal*. If we do something disapproved in one game, we may find ourselves sooner or later punished in another game.

This is essentially to say that a realistic version of the Tragedy of the Commons is more like an iterated, multi-player Prisoner's Dilemma in which the background conditions that make the Dilemma so unrealistic—and mathematically tractable— are dropped. We have some hunches about the other players' habits of thought and habits of social interaction, and can signal ours to them. We can punish, reward, or trust them later in many different social arenas, and they know this. In other words, the realistic background conditions are as complicated as our whole social life, including shared suspicions and mythology.

One of the early discoveries in the investigation of the idealized, iterated Prisoner's Dilemma was that the strategy of Tit-for-Tat is one of the most advantageous, simply described strategies.[12] This is a strategy of reprisals, in which you punish the other party for harming your stable, cooperative interests. Indeed, it is wise to pursue this strategy even if it is harmful for you in the short run, under certain conditions. This has been widely hailed in geopolitics as a kind of proof of the rationality of "realistic" policies of revenge, reprisal, and punishment that are often associated in the public mind with the vengeful politics of the Middle East or the Cold War. The implications of this superiority of the Tit-for-Tat strategy

---

12. See Kuhn's article in the *Stanford (Internet) Encyclopedia of Philosophy* and the literature he cites.

for real-world political and interpersonal affairs is far more complicated. Indeed, there are strategies that outperform Tit-for-Tat.[13]

THE DRIVE TO PRIVATIZE

Commentators who are friends of property and liberty undoubtedly view the Tragedy of the Commons as a dilemma that arises
with *any* mix of public and private goods. Because it is ethically or
politically wrong, or economically undesirable, or both, to make
everything public, everything—or as much as possible—must be
privatized.

Especially for those who defend a robust theory of private property on ethical grounds, such as from a theory of natural rights, it is
less clear where the "ought" arises to privatize the commons in the
first place—or the air, water, and so on. What is most clearly forbidden in such theories is the violation of anyone's present rights to
their current property. There are no rights for some individuals to
acquire property, such as what is now unowned. For one thing, this

---

13. See M. Nowak and K. Sigmund, "A Strategy of Win-stay, Lose-shift That
Outperforms Tit-for-tat in the Prisoner's Dilemma," *Nature*, 364 (July 1993):
76–81. The matter is extremely complicated and likely to produce future research—and surprises—because the notion of what counts as a "strategy" is difficult. *Simple* strategies that have been investigated base a response only on the
recent behavior of one's opponent, such as his last move. But there are an indef-
inite number of possible strategies, depending on how far back in the history of
play one goes to calculate one's next move. Human interaction can go very far
back, as in the phenomenon of holding a grudge or learning in childhood man-
ners and other "strategies" for social and intellectual success. Human interaction
can further incorporate cultural history and common sense stretching back many
times longer than a single human life—including the optimizing of a cultural
institution such as language. Given the impossibility of contemplating diverse and
mathematically described strategies of arbitrary lengths, and calculating their salience by running all combinations of outcomes, one might even propose that
commonality of human behaviors is the best available index of their salience,
since those large real-life strategies that are advantageous are more likely to be
retained (either because agents practicing it experience or realize it, or because of
a social Darwinism–sociobiology applied to cultural institutions).

would be a positive right and not merely a negative, prohibitive one. If we argue that someone has a right to acquire an unowned piece of property, the right would most likely arise from his or her need to develop their potential or nature. However, whatever this right-to-acquire is, it is then unclear why it wouldn't also count as a claim (though perhaps not always a dominant claim) to the use of property already owned by someone else

I must be very careful and clear here. I am agreeing to more or less unlimited use and rights to one's own property, legitimately acquired. What I am denying is a *right* to claim property as one's own. But while denying that there is a right to it, I am also not saying that it is wrong to acquire unowned property. It is neither one's right, nor is it wrong, to acquire property.[14] What counts as legitimate acquisition will most likely be culturally proscribed, as will be the "official" way of trading property. What counts as acquisition may have considerable variability, and many—but perhaps not all—means of doing so are neither (morally) "right" nor "wrong." I agree with some critics that there are defects in supposing that we can prove or derive that there is one rightful method, approved-for-all-cultures, to acquire property. This is the problem of what is called "original acquisition." The most famous constraint on original acquisition is Locke's, the so-called Lockean Proviso that such appropriation must leave enough for everyone else, and also leave this property in as good a condition as before (one cannot, for example, remove the bark from all trees). As David Schmidtz points out, there is as close to a "genuine consensus as views in political philosophy ever get" that this would undermine the possibility of *any* legitimate original acquisition.[15]

14. Compare David Schmidtz, "When Is Original Appropriation Required?" *The Monist*, 1990, pp. 504–18. Schmidtz speaks of appropriation being "justi-fied"—a somewhat ambiguous phrase to be sure, but compatible with my view that it is permissible and often convenient.
15. Ibid., pp. 504–5, citing critical views of Judith Jarvis Thompson, Jeremy

Another proposal (for example) makes original acquisition relative to one's intended purpose. If I am raising guinea pigs, I can stake a claim at most to several acres of land. If I am raising condors, I can lay claim to the whole state of California.[16] From such examples, we can see the folly in supposing that there is a natural right to acquisition by some ideal formula or other. We cannot and should not try to distinguish idealistic intent or outright delusion from a realistic intent. And we cannot easily identify specific goals as intrinsically better, that is, obviously falling within a correct vision of what is human nature to realize or become, and what it takes to accomplish this.[17]

There is no ideal basis by which we can define all proper original acquisition. Yet unlike many critics, I do not see that this limits or undermines rights to property, however they are acquired—so long as we have not violated others' rights. I believe it is necessary and *natural* to have rights to all objects one has made. This *making* is the essence of human flourishing, and will include a great deal. (It excludes that strangely vague Lockean notion of "mixing" labor with natural entities.) One does not have the right to any instrument one believes is helpful for that making—not automatically to tools others have made, manifestly, but neither does one have an automatic right to natural instruments for making things.[18] Some-

---

Waldron, Rolf Sartorius, and John T. Sanders. I am not convinced that Locke's view is so preposterous. For one thing, I think he could well have been contemplating an actual or hypothetical community in prehistory that was so small that land distribution was no problem (say, the first occupants of present-day Great Britain).

16. This was an example I once used against Murray Rothbard in Santa Barbara, California, some years ago. He was admirably unperturbed by it.

17. Although we might be able to exclude some goals as highly implausible, and qualify what is probably required for accomplishing some goals.

18. I here make reference to precise distinctions stated in my *Artifacts, Art Works, and Agency* (Philadelphia: Temple University Press, 1993). Tools are objects that have been intentionally modified by an agent to perform a function

what oddly for my account perhaps, one does not have a right to land, at least not a right to acquire it. One does have a right to what one has made on it, such as a house, and as a practical matter the physical integrity of the house might virtually require something akin to land ownership. Furthermore, I admit that one *may* (in some social circumstances) legitimately acquire land, although this is not a requirement of natural rights. That is a matter of local cultural conventions.

The only viable argument is not that individuals have a "right" to unowned property, or that it is in some strong ethical or political sense *obligatory* to privatize anything that can be identified and is reasonably scarce or could become so. Instead, it is desirable and efficient for a society to privatize many such entities. In careful formulations from the privatization wing, the language is often quite circumspect. Thus Machan argues that property is a precondition for (1) sovereignty and the exercise of moral responsibility, (2) for avoiding the Tragedy of the Commons, and (3) for the development of certain virtues.[19] Considerations (1) and (3) are arguably necessary for the flourishing of human nature. However, these claims are no argument for the extent of privatization. Developing these virtues and exercising moral responsibility might indeed require *some* private property, such as ownership of self and intentional human products. Furthermore, I think a developed version of my theory that "making" things is a crucial aspect of the flourishing of human nature would give far more support for private property, and perhaps even for some claims on the unowned means for this making, such as the commons. And while avoiding the Tragedy of the Commons is desirable, as I agree, this is not to

---

better; instruments are "natural" objects that already perform a function to some degree without such modification: a log as a chair, for example.

19. Tibor Machan, "A Defence of Property Rights and Capitalism," in Brenda Almond, ed., *Introducing Applied Ethics* (Cambridge: Blackwell, 1995).

argue that, since whatever avoids the Tragedy of the Commons is therefore morally obligatory, it follows that privatizing the commons is morally obligatory. There is instead at best an argument from prudence and efficiency.

COOPERATION WITHOUT PROPERTY

In my portrayal of the situation, the Right reaches for the "invisible hand" of Adam Smith to guide us to a better future and to avoid the Tragedy of the Commons. The Left reaches for the heavy hand of government. My own suggestion is that the invisible hand that guides us to efficient resource allocation through appropriating things as property, to which are then applied the benign laws of free-market economics, is not the only welcome hand. There is another invisible hand, what I shall call the *Deft Hand*, of informal social and interpersonal cooperation, that leads to very similar results. Strong evidence for its existence comes from the everyday way we punish and reward the behavior of others around us and from the common, informal tendencies to cooperate that show themselves in everything from language use to the grittier aspects of social conformity. An example is in philosophers believing in the supposedly secure logical foundations of democracy. Evidence of the long-term rationality of the Deft Hand is strongly suggested by the literature on various cooperative strategies in studies of iterated, multi-person Prisoner's Dilemmas.[20]

Another way of saying this is that because of human mental abilities, the deep rationality of cooperative strategies, and the evolution of human biological-social and cultural strategies, Tragedies

20. See, e.g., the classic Robert Axelrod, *The Evolution of Cooperation* (New York: Basic Books, 1984), as well as D. Kreps, J. Roberts and R. Wilson, "Rational Cooperation in the Finitely Repeated Prisoner's Dilemma," *Journal of Economic Theory* 27 (1982): 245–52 and A. Mukherji, V. Rajan, and J. Slagle, "Robustness of Cooperation," *Nature* 379 (January 1996): 125–26.

of the Commons are very rare. Where they do occur, we recover from them, and we have a wide variety of tools in our problem-solving kit that we can employ, of which "property" and original appropriation of it is just one example; perhaps mini-tragedies are even necessary so that there is pressure on us to devise cooperative strategies that will spare us the Big Tragedy.

Looked at in a certain broad perspective, property is just one kind of cooperative behavior. "Cooperative behavior" is intentional, joint action undertaken by two or more parties. Cooperative behavior is "formalized" if the intended behavior is governed by explicit rules or conditions. These might be written, or they might be part of clear and univocal customs and traditions understood by both parties (and each knows or has good reason to believe that the other party understands these conditions). In some cases, penalties for violating the conditions are also explicit, and the services of a third party such as the government or other contract-enforcement agency might guarantee these conditions. (This is itself another kind of cooperation.) This cooperative behavior may consist of permissions to do certain things (such as to use your property), obligations to do certain things (such as to pay my mortgage or give you a Christmas present too) or obligations to refrain from action (such as use of your property without explicit permission). In this sense, the institution of property is *a* formalized cooperative arrangement: we agree that I may use "my property" (permission) and we agree that you may not use it (prohibition). Most of these conditions are well understood and are indeed part of a written tradition (precedent or law).

Additionally, there is a huge array of nonformalized cooperative behaviors: an obligation to lend and a claim to borrow minor tools and condiments from neighbors, obligations to greet or return greetings, obligations to use words as others do, not to curse at them with little provocation, not to intervene casually but substantially in relationships that are to them intimate or vital, and so on.

Since they are not formalized and may be violated more or less freely (intentionally or by oversight), and depend in radical ways on convention and custom, perhaps it is wrong to call them "obligations." We could call them "cultural understandings" although I shall persist in calling them obligations—and I do not believe they always or necessarily come from shared cultural background (they can be individual understandings), and being a "mere" cultural tradition does not entail a lack of obligation. They are exceedingly weak obligations, to be sure. They may be violated in cases of even modest need, incompetence, or by oversight. Yet whatever appears to be a knowing or intentional violation of them permits retaliation—usually in kind, or at least "proportionally."

It is very important for political theorists to notice that there are a great many such cooperative understandings, that they too are necessary for civilization and life as we know it, that they are not matters of law or actions whose violation does, or should, warrant the use of force. It is perhaps important for individual psychological development, and for rapid cultural progress, that many of these "necessary" cooperative arrangements *not* be formalized. In any case, to formalize all of them—like the dating arrangements at Antioch College—is unnecessary, practically impossible, and probably wrong. This trivial and I think obvious proposition is important for blocking the necessity of privatizing the commons. Even where a state of affairs is more efficient and "better" for all parties, this does not mean that this state of affairs should be—or even is permitted to be—mandated by formalized cooperative behavior, such as is provided by the institution of private property or by state regulation.

Although it is beyond the scope of this essay to describe in more detail the exact nature of cooperative behavior, or the "natural kinds" of it, it is important to reflect briefly on some of the reasons why we engage in it. First, we might both be better off, in a direct and obvious way, if we engage in this behavior. We might not be able to accomplish a task, such as moving a fallen tree from the road, without joint effort. This raises the expected outcome for both of us. Second, we might be able to avoid harmful states from befalling one of us (not yet identified) if we cooperate, such as exhibiting a readiness to lend a tool or help a neighbor in an emergency. Finally, we might be able to avoid harm to both of us that could arise from uncoordinated or uncontrolled separate efforts—this is the case of the commons.

Each different motivation tends to have its own distinctive form of cooperative behavior, and each has its own variety of "free rider" problem. What is often sloppily called the free rider is actually a cluster of cases of unfulfilled cooperative behavior. Such cases typically arise (only) when we cannot determine who is not fulfilling their cooperative obligation, or when there are not enough mutual cooperative understandings so that we can retaliate against known violators in a serious way. Hence I do not see the Tragedy of the Commons as being similar to the free rider problem, since there were not cooperative arrangements for the use of the commons already in place. (One variant proposes that a herdsman sneaks into the commons at night to allow his large herd to graze, but his very "sneaking" indicates a belief that he understands that there *is* a cooperative arrangement, and then the problem is a garden-variety problem of enforcement.)

Throughout this discussion, I am not assuming that we are or should be altruists. Instead, I think it is simply rational to be inclined to a relatively indiscriminant altruism or "cooperation," once we understand the huge and diverse array of cooperative understandings, most of them unformalized and little discussed, that are integral parts of civilized life. (This point is further driven home if we also realize that Tit-for-Tat's superiority as a rational strategy is a mathematical fact.)[21] There is thus something seriously amiss in Ayn

---

21. Or some similar retaliatory-rewarding-signaling strategy.

Rand's rhetoric of the "virtue of selfishness": it seems not to grasp the large number of largely unformalized cooperative arrangements that are already in place, and are in fact necessary for civilization, and it instead takes seriously only formalized cooperative arrangements, such as written contracts. It ignores the diversity and depth of human cooperative behaviors (perhaps themselves stemming from human nature) and it seeks to legalize those few it does acknowledge.

THE RETURN OF SHAME

It is curious, and should be surprising to most political philosophers, that in various local and regional short-term water shortages, compliance with prohibitions against watering the lawn or washing cars is more often gained by fear of neighbors' sentiments than by the Water Police. It is an almost primal fear of "the Stare" of Societal Noncompliance, more common and highly perfected in Central Europe, that does the work. One fears one's children being berated by neighbors' children as coming from "that kind of family." One fears the frown, and remark—and one does not act clearly, rationally, and exactly, from fear of the law and police alone. It is shame and stigma that do the work. One can think of many similar cases. Mowing the lawn, reducing weeds, keeping dog's excrement off of private property (less successfully off of sidewalks and park greens), keeping out of the passing lane if driving slowly, not tailgating, and so on for a wide variety of publicly observable behaviors that have a clear impact on others. Compliance is most widely achieved by informal social agreements and their associated vague societal pressures—with the frown, the stare, the remark, stigmatizing deviant's children, and so on, all of which count as cross-modal Tit-for-Tat strategies. Laws and their enforcement agents are rarely utilized; rather, we behave within the law not so much to avoid punishment or a fine but out of awareness of the social myth of uniformed intervention and the shame of being seen being arrested. (I would conjecture that this is the main factor behind the threshold phenomenon in unusual and socially noncompliant behaviors: with large numbers of defectors, stares lose their sting or are impractical.) In Europe, the shame factor and enforcement myth works quite well in public transportation; in New York City, it is unimaginable.

Shame is a distinctive feeling of being seen by others in one's society as doing something known to be disapproved of; a barely distinguishable feeling is *imagining* being seen doing this.[22] It is related to embarrassment, but embarrassment is often weaker and is in my usage felt not because of knowledge of doing something disapproved of, but because of sometimes imagined failings to conform to normalcy. If someone notices how gangly I am, that my bathing suit has slipped an inch or two, or that my socks are mismatched, then I am embarrassed but not in my sense "ashamed." Both are distinct from moral guilt, because in guilt I do not need even to imagine others observing my deed to have the feeling and (arguably) there is a conception of a trans-societal standard. There are variants of these "behavioral-normative" feelings, as well as still other ones—such as sin.

Shame is seen quite clearly in customs of ritual cleanliness that we encounter in ancient Judaism or Romany (Gypsy) culture. In this form, it is often given a sensuous dimension, and is associated with an offense to the eyes or—even more often—to smell. (European vs. American issues of hygiene, antiperspirants, body hair, and proper levels of bodily exposure evoke confused cross-cultural notions of shame and judgment.) This visceral component is not always present, and we sometimes have only a diffuse stigma: of

22. See R. Jay Wallace, *Responsibility and the Moral Sentiments* (Cambridge, Mass.: Harvard University Press, 1994), especially pp. 37–40 for what Wallace calls "moral reactive attitudes." See also *Pride, Shame, and Guilt: Emotions of Self-Assessment* (Oxford: Clarendon Press, 1985) for a somewhat more careful discussion. My own notion of shame differs from Wallace's.

being *that* kind of person, in some pejorative sense. It more often attaches to one's character or whole being than simply to transient acts. It is a judgment-like feeling about an agent rather than about an act. (Embarrassment and guilt are frequently act-notions; sin may be either.) In the postwar American era, shame has acquired a uniformly bad rap. Shame has made a slow return among neoconservatives. Thus Marvin Olasky, one source of George W. Bush's "compassionate conservatism," writes sarcastically in his *The Tragedy of American Compassion* that the key contribution of the War on Poverty was unfortunately to "uncouple welfare from shame."[23] It is a widespread view of those born after World War II, and of other enlightened people, that society should not be able to make one feel bad just for violating its standards.

It is true that traditional shame cultures have often had a repressive and authoritarian character. Are there proper and improper—even immoral—codes of shame? What is the proper province of formal cooperative arrangements, as opposed to informal ones such as those governed by shame? These are extremely complicated questions, while my purpose here has been only to induce the reader to see a whole new dimension of social life, one that may solve the Tragedy of the Commons in many cases. I think cooperative arrangements should generally be informal rather than formal; this is to balk at excessive legalization. Exceptions to this occur when the offending behavior is an especially serious violation of rights of others that justifies the fallible institutions of enforcement that then arise, and especially when the offending behavior is by its nature not publicly observable. Shame, too, has its limits in a good society: one should have a free choice of the system of shame one chooses (right to emigrate and immigrate across national or subcultural boundaries) and shame should generally be restricted to bringing individuals' conformance in cases of clear and reasonable dam-

---

23. Quoted in the *New York Times*, June 12, 2000, p. A24.

age to others' interests. Scorning (but perhaps not outlawing) public nudity is a "reasonable" use of shame, but forbidding private sex acts is not.[24]

In a modern industrial society in which some offending behaviors may be performed by corporations, I view boycotts as a reasonable and proper action. Alas, those who would promote boycotts (environmentalists, for example) are often those who are against all forms of shame. Consequently, the rhetoric of their campaign does not reach deeply enough into human practices and psychology. To be effective, we must be able to view some companies, and all who work for them and buy from them, as "dirty" or otherwise fiercely stigmatized. Like geopolitical reprisals, this may superficially appear nasty and unkind.

There are very good reasons for believing that coordinated behaviors in a satisfactorily ordered society must be achieved without depending only on moral duty and guilt (too weak) and law (too clumsy and heavy-handed). These are informal morally reactive sentiments like shame itself, embarrassment, or sin. (However, overreliance on the requisite standard of "normalcy" for embarrassment will have a stultifying effect, such as the society pilloried in the 1950's dystopic film *Pleasantville*.) The difficulty with morality, tied so closely to rationality, is that many desirable (even necessary) coordinated behaviors do not have a rational basis, such as why we *should* drive on the right-hand side of the road, or why words *should* be used in the way they are. It is often important that we agree upon one behavioral regularity, but far less important which it is.[25] There is thus a kind of higher rationality, which Douglas Hofstadter dubs superrationality, that favors the uniform adoption of "irra-

---

24. The only author I know with a carefully calibrated and morally defensible attitude both to conventions and to "proper" notions of shame is Montaigne, such as in his essay on nakedness.

25. Rituals for acquiring and transferring property might belong here, too.

tional" codes as "conventions."[26] There is a positive value, even a wisdom, in some forms of irrational conformism that have uniformly been anathema since the 1960s and also run counter to some extreme (and to my mind shallow and thoughtless) libertarian ideals of individualism. Reflection upon the conventions of language[27] rapidly brings one to such conclusions, and thus explain the cultural "conservatism" of thinkers such as Wittgenstein.

A final example. I would have to admit that although its means are not fully morally sanctioned (as obligatory), the option of privatizing the commons is both morally permissible and effective in avoiding the Tragedy of the Commons. My main hesitation in promoting privatization arises from my preference for less heavy-handed cooperative arrangements. However, there is one infamous case in political theory where, for a variety of reasons, an instance of the commons cannot be privatized.

This is the case of children. They cannot—*should* not—literally be owned.[28] Behavior toward them should be constrained in numerous ways. But they are not themselves full agents with all rights of citizenry. They do not "have" rights in the sense in which morally autonomous adults do, yet they are not just the property of their parents, to be treated however parents wish so long as they don't infringe on other adults' wishes. Political theory has, about the notable issue of children's education in an election year, very little of substance to say about this difficult problem. Privatizing education doesn't alone solve the problem, since it does not solve the problem of whether parents have the right to decide what education their children receive without any constraint. Speaking of them as bearers of rights in virtue of their potential future agency is likewise fraught with difficulty.

26. Douglas Hofstadter, *Metamagical Themas* (New York: Basic Books, 1985).
27. These extensive nonrational but desirable elements of human life have not been pursued much after David Lewis's fine book, *Convention*.
28. As we typically understand property.

One option is to institute formal cooperative institutions, such as laws governing negative and positive obligations toward children. This works well enough for parental obligations governing basic health and welfare, such as food. (The source of even these obligations is nevertheless somewhat mysterious.) But how do we control parents who would pack their innocent children's head full of psychotic nonsense, dress them in costumes so they are laughed at, or forbid them from reading books? I see here almost a unique necessity for a robust notion of shame. Any society worthy of the name will bring shame down upon such parental deviants—voluntarily and extensively, so that such deviants will find no job, no friends, no conversation, and will be effectively shunned.

WHY THE GIMMICKS?

I now return to the issue that began this discussion. It is easily expressed: why the gimmicks in political philosophy? That is, why does political philosophy make more appeals, compared with other branches of philosophy and other disciplines, to a variety of implausible, hypothetical, or highly idealized scenarios? To be sure, not all traditions in political philosophy do this. We see the use of artificial devices or implausible scenarios in Plato, the Modern tradition of Hobbes and Locke, and then again in the post–World War II era. We typically do not see them in Aristotle,[29] the medieval tradition, and generally in the Natural Law tradition of ethics and politics.

My explanation for this unusual phenomenon is this. Political philosophy, as well as ethics, is a supremely difficult field. It requires a deep understanding of little-understood psychological, economic, and social features of human beings. (In its more fine-tuned and

---

29. I see a hint of an artificial scenario that supposedly defines an issue at one place in Aristotle: the beginning of Book VIII of the *Nicomachean Ethics* on the transcendent importance of friendship.

individualistic apparition, it requires a deep appreciation of the nature of deliberation, rationality, intention, and action. While we have some good guesses and promising theories, there is no consensus, nor are there in these domains deep, satisfactory, agreed-upon, precise accounts.[30]) Problems in political philosophy also interact with the hardest of philosophical problems, on which there is little or no agreement. Are there objective values? What ultimately exists—in particular, do things such as human beings have (*de re* rather than merely *de dicto*) "natures or essences"? How are mental states related to physical circumstances? What counts as knowledge and do we have it about propositions of relevance to politics and ethics?

Yet, few have been satisfied with politics as a highly tentative, pure theoretical enterprise. Political philosophers, at least many of them, have been eager to inject their intuitions and views into the real political realm—to convince people that their views, or at least their conclusions, are true, and will, if believed or at least acquiesced to, lead to a happier life for all. But how can we do this, when the arguments are so weak, the relevant theoretical facts speculative and not agreed upon, and the overall grip on a whole theory of ethics so tentative and debatable? What almost everyone reaches for in this situation is, I believe, to turn to *motivational intellectual devices*. We forge a consensus on some contours of a desirable relationship of state to citizen merely by getting enough people to agree that a certain account is plausible or attractive. This is not really philosophy as we normally and ideally understand it. It is a kind of manipulative pedagogy, a gentle persuasion of the body politic. We can see that agreement and acquiescence to common

---

30. Action theory is rather undeveloped compared with theories of perception and the other merely passive aspects of thinking and understanding, such as phenomenology and epistemology. One sees efforts to inject a more action-influenced approach to "inquiry" in the works of Peirce and Dewey.

beliefs alone have some very great value, never mind *to what*.[31] We avoid the state of nature, and have a point of leverage that brings verbal acquiescence or acknowledgment of "rightful" moral, political, or intellectual power—at least in many cases—without the need for more brutal forms of force. But those scrappy intellectuals! They see this too, but cannot be counted upon to agree to plebeian stories about the gods, the wisdom of the ancients, and all the hoary traditional devices of fiction or myth.[32] They need their own, more complicated and typically secular "stories," without which they are intellectually affronted. These are the highly artificial, idealized, or hypothetical devices of political theory—which themselves require a wink and a nod, but at a very lofty intellectual level.

The modes of appealing to this nonplebeian self-conception of intellectual integrity are various. They can be mathematized or technical accounts like calculations of resources and growth (Malthus), various optimizing equilibria and saddle points, Prisoner's Dilemmas, or Arrow's Theorem. They can be "hypothetical" scenarios involving an abstraction of ideal rationality—mixing folk history and widespread but not carefully articulated views of human nature or of counterfactual inclinations. Or they can be artful and tricky cases, typically against the background of criticizing some previous ethical or political theory and almost always underdescribed in leaving out what may well be, but are not obviously, salient facts in the ethical and political context. These "counterexamples" are typically regarded by a kind of institutional consensus as being especially probing and accomplished (in their professional

---

31. Peirce has the wisdom to see that this is so even for methods of fixing of belief that are purely authoritative, and generally despised. See "The Fixation of Belief" (1877) in *Writings of Charles S. Peirce: A Chronological Edition*, vol. 3 (Bloomington: Indiana University Press, 1986), pp. 250–51.

32. There is an urging to return to narrative, artistic, and fictional expositions of morals by Martha Nussbaum (*The Fragility of Goodness*), William Bennett (*The Book of Virtues*), and Bernard Williams (*Shame and Necessity*).

context), and therefore as being the new ideas on which the next barely plausible theory can be constructed and advanced as "surely" right-minded.

Unlike the current fashion in ethical and political discourse of being above it all and "posttheoretical," I am not counseling that we should avoid efforts to create substantive theory. In fact, I see no reason for being pessimistic about the "ontological" condition of these disciplines; I think there are almost certainly real truths about the nature of the world and man, and "true," objective values about the best ethical and political values and arrangements. Nor am I a Kantian pessimist who believes that human grasping of these noumenal truths is in principle impossible and that no progress has been or can be made. My quibble is with how the epistemological status of various claims in contemporary political theory is precisely portrayed; it is with the widespread pretense of factuality and logicality that is especially widespread in analytical ethics and political philosophy.

There are some political traditions that avoid this collective delusion of right-mindedness. The natural law tradition does this, as do some neo-Hegelian traditions (such as Michael Oakshott's). They acknowledge, implicitly if not explicitly, the complex and intertwined nature of their own conceptions. They do not pretend to have achieved "clean" and precise notions. If they err, it is where they move from expansive but murky (and in details, fallible) theories to a self-assured advocacy for actual political arrangements. While tentatively libertarian, I find the usual Libertarianism repugnant as a belief with claims to *knowledge*. However, given the desirability for us all of some consensus on basic features of government and ethics,[33] the overexpansive rhetoric of even these more restrained advocates is arguably justifiable on pragmatic grounds. Fur-

---

33. There are some similarities of my views with David Gauthier, *Morals by Agreement* (Oxford: Clarendon Press, 1986).

thermore, because of my keen awareness of the grave epistemological shortcomings of all current political philosophy—and similar weakness in deep thought about any truly difficult subjects—I am especially interested in "minimal" such fabrications that are likely to do the least harm. Advocates for ethical, political, and educational prescriptions should be especially mindful of the ancient Hippocratic wisdom first to avoid doing harm.[34]

34. I detect in my recent views some influence of the ideas of my friends Avrum Stroll and Nicholas Capaldi, ideas to which I was initially hostile.

CHAPTER THREE

Ending the Environmental Tragedy of the Commons

Richard L. Stroup
and
Jane S. Shaw

DURING THE SECOND HALF of the twentieth century, economists became increasingly aware of the role of common ownership in causing environmental problems. The "tragedy of the commons" is now a familiar way to frame them. It explains the classic examples of overexploitation such as excessive fishing and overuse of grazing land, and it is also a way of understanding air and water pollution.

Economists have long recognized the problems posed by commonly owned property rights, and in 1954, H. Scott Gordon outlined the concept of the "tragedy of the commons" in explaining the decline of a fishery (Gordon 1954). However, at first, economists did not apply this insight widely.

Economists paid little attention to the commons problem in part because they viewed environmental problems such as pollution and overexploitation as minor, both for society and for the economics profession. In addition, most economists thought that the British economist A. C. Pigou had successfully addressed environmental problems when he developed the concept of externalities introduced by Alfred Marshall (Pigou 1960 [1932]). Someone engages in a lawful activity such as manufacturing a product, but allows waste—smoke or chemicals or heavy metals—to enter the air or water. Because the pollution is outside the market transaction, external to the people producing and purchasing the product, it is an externality, and the people affected—those who bear the cost—are third parties. Conceptually, Pigou had a fairly simple way of dealing with externality: government intervention. The government should place a tax or levy on the pollution so that the producer would pay the cost and therefore have an incentive to diminish the harm.

The neglect of the problem of common property ended around the middle of the century. Ronald Coase, who won a Nobel Prize in economics in 1991, wrote a paper that in effect challenged Pigou's concept of externalities and helped launch a broad reconsideration of property rights (Coase 1960). Coase argued that if the action of one person harms another, as in the case of pollution, this should be viewed as a problem between two parties, not as an externality. Either one—the polluter or the one affected by the pollution—can act to reduce the harm. If the polluter has the legal right to pollute, the person harmed may still pay the polluter not to do so, or the polluter might move the harmed activity elsewhere to avoid damages. If the victim has the right not to be harmed, the polluter may either stop the pollution or pay the victim to allow it. Coase's article focused the discussion of pollution on property rights, productive trading, and the bargaining (or "transactions") costs that might stifle such trades.

Then in 1968, Hardin's famous article was published in *Science* magazine (Hardin 1979 [1968], 16–30). A biologist, not an economist, Hardin popularized the concept of the "tragedy of the commons" throughout many disciplines. Although Hardin did not endorse private property rights as the preferred solution, his framing of the issue gave new life to the ideas of ownership and nonownership and their application to environmental issues. Hardin's essay appeared just as modern environmental concern (celebrated in Earth Day 1970) was emerging, and it reached a broad audience.

THE LOGIC OF THE COMMONS

Hardin discussed a village commons. He proposed that when a common pasture is not owned by an individual or a single decision-making unit (and thus no one has the authority to control access to it) deterioration of the commons is inevitable if the village continues to grow. A villager deciding how many cows to graze on an open-access common pasture will seek primarily the welfare of himself and his family, rather than seeking to understand and give equal weight to the more far-reaching effects through time of that decision on all others. In a commons that has reached its carrying capacity, the benefit to the individual from the addition of one cow is far more than the costs, because the costs are spread across all the villagers. This leads to overexploitation and even depletion because the costs of exploitation to each individual are less than the costs placed upon others in the society. Only when the resource is vast in comparison to potential human demands for it is overexploitation unlikely.

The commons has implications for many resources such as grazing land and wildlife, and air and water can be viewed as a commons as well. In "The Tragedy of the Commons" and a later essay (Hardin 1993) Hardin identifies three logical possibilities for correcting the problems of the commons: private ownership in a market system, government-imposed rules, and traditional customs. In the last case, if a resource is owned in common by a small and cohesive group, monitoring of use and social pressure can prevent overexploitation. Social pressure, Hardin observes, probably cannot be effective alone when group size goes beyond about 150 people (ibid., 90).

To correct the problem of the commons one must choose

among the available alternatives. The choice is primarily between private property and government control, since traditional customs are difficult to develop spontaneously or by fiat.

In order to make a wise choice, one has to recognize (as Tibor Machan discusses in the Introduction to this volume) that the need for institutional influence over the control of resources exists even in the absence of selfishness, for even selfless individuals, as decision makers, are inherently limited to a narrow view that can lead to overuse or other kinds of exploitation.[1]

Both the chief executive officer of General Motors, seeking a larger share of auto market profits, and a saintly nun like the late Mother Teresa, seeking succor for the ill and destitute in Calcutta, tend to make decisions within the narrow focus of special goals. These goals are so important to them that consideration of other, broader goals, such as preservation of a wilderness or research toward a cure for cancer, will at best be given secondary importance. Each person will consider the broader effects only to the degree that institutional forces provide information about the effect of the decision on others and offer an incentive to act on that information.

Yet to solve the tragedy of the commons, each decision about resource use must take into consideration the desires of others, including potential future users of the resource. Because each person will, by and large, follow narrow personal goals, the ability to use those resources in the future depends on the alignment of personal goals with those of others in society. This essay will discuss each choice.

THE GOVERNMENTAL CHOICE

Increasingly over the past one hundred years, the typical way of dealing with a commons—grazing land, parks, and air and water

---

1. Some of the observations that follow were initially discussed in Stroup 1991.

pollution—has been to turn it over to governmental regulation. This is the "mutual coercion, mutually agreed upon by the majority of the people affected" that Hardin refers to in his 1968 essay, although he insists that this does not have to mean distant bureaucrats (Hardin 1977, 27). The experience of government control of the environment has in many respects been a dismal one.

Perhaps the most dramatic disappointment comes from the classic example of the commons, overfishing. In 1976, the United States government took control of fishing for numerous species with the passage of the Magnuson Fishery Conservation and Management Act. Yet a 1999 report by the National Marine Fisheries Service identified 98 species as overfished (experiencing fewer or smaller fish each year) and another five species as nearing an overfished condition. For 674 fish species, or 75 percent of all species it reviewed, the agency simply did not know whether they were overfished or not (Leal 2000, 1).

More broadly, governmental control of air and water pollution (which expanded dramatically with national legislation in 1970) has been costly and in many respects ineffective. Research by Indur Goklany (1999) has concluded that by the time the Clean Air Act Amendments of 1970 were passed, ambient levels of the key pollutants that the legislation targeted (particulates, sulfur dioxide, ozone, and carbon monoxide) had already been declining. Control by the Environmental Protection Agency did not speed up the decline.

For water, Goklany (1996) observes that by the time the Clean Water Act (1972) and the Safe Drinking Water Act (1974) were adopted the most serious water-related environmental problems, access to safe drinking water and adequate sanitation, had been largely solved. The actual impact of the national legislation is difficult to discern because the government did not have baseline measurements of the quality of water in the United States in 1972 and has never adopted a consistent set of comprehensive water quality data (Avery and Halpern 2000). Summarizing the effect of national

environmental regulations, a recent textbook by Harvard economist W. Kip Viscusi and others concluded that the high expectations "for the most part . . . were not fulfilled" (Viscusi, Vernon,
and Harrington 1997, 655).

For other commons that have been replaced by government
control, such as national parks and forests, a growing literature is
revealing wasteful management, ecological deterioration, and a
harmful short-term focus by government officials. Forests are in-
fested with insects and ready to go up in flames, biodiversity in our
national parks is declining, and many park managers do not even
know the actual state of their natural resources (Chase 1986; Leal
and Fretwell 1997; Fretwell 1999a, 1999b).

REASONS FOR GOVERNMENT FAILURE

Why is governmental control a poor alternative to the commons?
The answer begins with the fact that, as we indicated earlier in
reference to the head of General Motors and to Mother Teresa, all
people pursue the goals that matter the most to them. Inevitably,
they ignore or disregard many goals that others value. Individuals
do not give up these narrow interests when they join government,
an observation that public choice scholars have substantiated over
the past few decades (see, for example, Mitchell and Simmons
1994). In fact, each program in each agency serves narrow goals.

Second, many characteristics of government, even a democracy,
lead government officials to pursue those narrow interests without
taking into account the goals of many other groups and other government programs (Gwartney, Stroup, and Sobel 2000; Wolf
1988). Supreme Court Justice Stephen Breyer has labeled this
problem "tunnel vision," a "classic administrative disease" in which
an employee "carries single-minded pursuit of a single goal too far,
to the point where it brings about more harm than good" (Breyer
1993, 11).

The government itself is like a commons. Policies aimed at protecting the public interest are "owned in common." This gives government actors many opportunities to pursue their narrow interests—for example, building dams or supporting farm prices—without considering the effects of those actions on others in society. The policies that benefit the narrow interests or goals of persons in government (specific groups of voters, bureaucrats, and politicians) may not benefit the public as a whole.

Defining exactly how the public as a whole benefits is problematic, of course. People have such diverse goals that few collective actions can provide them all with benefits. Economists often claim that the chief goal of an economy is to promote "general economic well-being" (Mankiw 1998, 9), and they view the government as having a role in achieving this well-being. We recognize, however, that "economic well-being" differs among individuals, so that there is no single goal for all people. Even so, it is better for individuals and their agents to be more concerned about the goals of others than to ignore them. The problem of the commons is that it leads individuals to ignore the wishes of others.

The Role of the Voter

To understand the problems of government control of resources, we begin with the heart of democratic government, the voter, whose wishes are supposed to be represented by government officials. Voters, however, do a poor job of directing and monitoring government action. One reason is the voter's rational ignorance.

Each voter knows that his or her vote will not be decisive. (Economist Gordon Tullock points out that statistically the voter driving to the polls is more likely to be killed in an auto accident along the way than to cast the deciding vote.)[2] In this situation,

2. Tullock said this in conversation with one of the authors.

there is little incentive for the individual to spend time, effort, and hard thought in seeking added knowledge about the policies, or even the candidates, in question. The costs of informed voting are high and the benefit is low because the individual voter has a minuscule impact on the election. The voter's choice probably depends more on conscience and the entertainment value of the process than on the expected effect of the vote.

So, although the voter may be quite intelligent, he or she does not find that it makes sense to obtain sufficient information to monitor the political process closely, except perhaps in the case of his or her narrow special interests or concerns. Polls show that the average American of voting age cannot even name his or her congressional representative; this result has been consistent across decades and across states. Owners of high-sulfur coal mines know well the effects of the Clean Air Act on the burning of their coal, but most citizens who simply breathe the air know very little about these issues. They cannot be informed voters and thus cannot effectively influence or monitor their elected representatives on most issues.

Even if the voter could overcome rational ignorance, the "bundle purchase" problem limits the voter's ability to express his or her wishes. A voter normally votes for a political representative, not for each policy option separately. The winning candidate will represent the voters on thousands of issues each legislative session, and each voter must accept one candidate's bundle of future votes (most of which the voter will know nothing about). Voters' influence is extremely imprecise, even in a representative democracy.

Lack of Accountability

In government, as in any commons, costs are very widely shared. Normally, no one citizen can be held accountable for the adoption or execution of a specific policy; the responsibility for making and monitoring policy is diluted. A government official has a strong incentive to pursue his or her narrow goals as long as this pursuit does not run afoul of the voters. Since the voter is largely uninformed and probably unaware of an action unless it makes headlines, the official has a great deal of leeway as long as negative headlines are avoided. The payoff to pleasing (or at least not seriously displeasing) voters encourages "spin"—using the official organs of information and the press to give the best possible picture (the picture most popular with voters) of an action that in fact was intended to achieve the official's narrow goals.

The somewhat monopolistic position of each agency reinforces the government official's lack of incentive to take into account the effects—especially the long-term effects—on others of a policy decision. Voters cannot easily shift their support to a competing agency because there is rarely a competitor trying to achieve similar results for the public. (Agencies could, in fact, be set up to compete so that the more efficient can achieve growth at the expense of the less efficient. But what politician will fight hard for this option against a hostile bureaucracy wanting no competitors? The benefits would be spread widely among voters, most of whom haven't even thought about the issue.)

There is an exception to the "no headlines" policy. The "Washington Monument strategy" can operate instead. The name comes from Washington, D.C., where the Washington Monument is one of the most popular attractions on the Mall. Threats of budget cuts (or increases less than requested by an agency) can cause an agency such as the National Park Service to react by threatening to shorten hours at the most popular government facility that agency controls—in the case of the Park Service, the George Washington monument. Though all federal agencies (and local ones as well) use this technique, it is particularly effective with the National Park Service. In 1996, the Park Service closed a museum and two campgrounds in Yellowstone National Park. These facilities have been profitable, but because the income from fees went to the national treasury, not to Yellowstone Park, the operating costs of the museum and the campground were a drain on the Yellowstone budget. The closing of the facilities raised quite an outcry (Fretwell 1999b, 9). Subsequently, the park received an additional $1.8 million appropriation from Congress, an increase that Yellowstone Park officials credit to the closing down.[3]

This lack of accountability is especially detrimental with respect to action that affects the future. It is a common aphorism that the long-term future for a politician extends to the next election.[4] The government decision maker has little incentive to fight for long-run goals that run counter to present-day pressures. Bureaucratic and political decision makers cannot benefit personally from increasing the future value of the resources they are entrusted with. Unlike private owners, whose assets can rise in value, a government official cannot earn a financial profit by successfully fighting for a future policy payoff while the costs are in the present. Concomitantly, government officials lack the accountability that comes from the loss of personal wealth when the future value of the resource declines.

To illustrate this problem, one has only to look at the management of forests. Good sylvan management will increase the wealth of a private forest owner. But for the government official in charge of a similar forest, there is no direct reward for careful management and therefore less incentive to exercise it. Wildfires around Los Alamos, New Mexico, during the spring of 2000 (highly publicized in the media) illustrate poor management as well as the fragmentation of responsibility. Although one Park Service official (the fire started on a Park Service national monument but moved to Forest

3. Don Striker, then Comptroller of Yellowstone Park, stated this on October 1, 1999.
4. Ironically, many people often expect government officials to be more farsighted than private owners.

Service land) was put on leave, the "CEO" of the Interior Department, Bruce Babbitt, kept his job. Eventually the problem disappeared from the headlines. As long as Babbitt could ride out the immediate political storm, neither he nor anyone else had to account for the failure. Later in the year, more fires spread through the West. Indeed, the Forest Service has about 40 million acres of old, insect-infested trees that could go up in flames some time soon (General Accounting Office 1999). Because no one's personal future or fortune is at stake, the problem is unlikely to be solved. Solutions would be costly, and some of the cost would be borne by those seeking to improve conditions. Why fight that battle? No Forest Service official will be rewarded for maintaining or restoring the future quality of the forests.

Rent Seeking

Government control leads to favor seeking (economists call it rent seeking) or political predation by special interests. As we have seen, the voter is a poor monitor for the public interest because the individual's costs of monitoring (obtaining relevant information) are high in relation to the personal benefits. However, many voters have specific goals that they can use government to achieve. By banding together to lobby as well as to vote, such special interests can take advantage of the ignorance of the voter and of the lack of focused responsibility that is typical of government. Using government's coercive powers, they can obtain benefits at the expense of others. Small organized interests with concentrated goals gain at the expense of the unorganized majority because the cost of each predation is small when dispersed across a large population. (To control this tendency, the U.S. Constitution was written in ways that limited the domain of government power, but over time court decisions have weakened the restrictions.)

Injustice

Another sign that government officials may be pursuing goals desired by some at the expense of others is the fact that government
agencies tend to serve the relatively powerful and wealthy.)[5] The
same skills and activities that lead to high incomes will lead to
greater political clout. The national parks, for example, are supported primarily by taxpayers, not by park fees, which are low
relative to the travel cost paid by most visitors. Yet park visitors
appear to have incomes nearly double those of the average taxpayers who subsidize their visits (Economic Staff 1980). The Park
Service subsidizes the Kennedy Center in Washington, D.C., with
several million dollars each year even though the average attendee
has an income far above that of the average taxpayer. Special "VIP"
facilities in parks are closed to most citizens. In contrast, private
facilities such as McDonald's, facing stiff and direct competition,
woo people who have relatively little money and arguably treat
them better than do those pulling the levers that control government.

Taken together, these characteristics explain why many government policies do not achieve their stated goals, including environmental goals, and why the government's powers are so often used

---

5. The Constitution limited the ability of special interests (then called "fac-
tions") to practice political predation. Erosion of these limits, however, has led to
the growth of transfer activities. From the mid-1950s to 1975, the U.S. federal
government grew from about 24 percent of GNP to about 36 percent. This
increase represents a rise in transfers; none of it went to increase the purchase of
goods and services. Of this remarkable increase in transfers, nearly all—five dollars
in every six—were not means-tested. Thus, owing to the political influence of
special interest groups, most transfers are not earmarked for poor people. Survey
data consistently show that low-income people know less about political issues,
vote less, and are less politically active than people with higher incomes. Politicians who wish to survive in the competitive political arena will pay attention
primarily to those who know more about the issues, and who vote.

to further the interests of narrow, but politically well organized, groups.

In contrast to government control, private property rights and trade harness the narrow interests of individuals toward goals desired by all who bear the costs. When private property rights are well defined, well protected, and transferable, all those in the economy tend to benefit, for several reasons:

- The person who wants to use a product or resource must pay for it by outbidding others who want it. Thus, the creation of value is rewarded by those who, in their own judgment, will benefit.

- The cost of degrading a resource is paid by the one who degrades it. The owner who spoils the future use of land through pollution or overexploitation may experience the reduced value of the land, either in the form of reduced income from the land through his or her period of ownership or in a lower sale price to a future owner—who of course stands to lose income also.

- A person who degrades someone else's property can be sued by the owner to stop the harm and to collect for damages already done. Both parties have an incentive to avoid or stop this situation—the one who is tempted to degrade someone else's property knows that the courts will stop it and the one who would suffer the degradation fights it because it will reduce the property's value. This system, with each paying the cost of what he or she does, provides incentives to conserve and to protect natural resources and to avoid environmental damage.

Adam Smith, the founder of classical economics, recognized that when interaction is based on voluntary exchange, individual desires are channeled, as if by an "invisible hand," into activities that are beneficial to others in the society. An individual may not care deeply about others' goals but will prosper in a market setting if he or she acts *as if* the happiness of others matters. The president of a major company may be a cranky misanthrope, but in a competitive market he or she seeks to make the company's customers happy with the firm's products and services. The better the executive is at doing this, the more successful the company will be and the more the executive will be rewarded. Both the incentives and the information necessary to consider the needs of others are provided in the marketplace.

Market Participants

While voters remain uninformed about candidates and issues because the cost of being informed would far outweigh the benefit to them, participants in markets are decisive in their own purchase and investment choices: they actually get what they pay for, whereas voters do not necessarily get what they vote for. Market participants achieve their goals by using resources that are costly to them. The more efficiently they use those resources, the more they achieve what they want.

This self-serving process has a benefit to others because it leads to efficient use of resources and to their long-term protection. In other words, it counters the overexploitation of the commons and the waste of resources.

The information and incentives that market participants need to make value-producing, resource-conserving decisions come in large measure through market prices. When prices go up, buyers consume less; when prices are low, they consume more. Thus buyers economize more when goods are more scarce, allowing others who are willing to sacrifice more to consume more of the goods. When goods are plentiful and there is a lot to go around, buyers purchase more.

For example, each consumer of electricity, seeking his or her narrow goals and responding to prices, chooses whether or not to use heat and air conditioning and how high or low to set the thermostat. Although consumers may not concern themselves with others' needs, by consuming less when prices are high they make scarce electricity more available for others. Conservation in this way helps to keep prices from going still higher and may gradually bring them down. The seller responds to prices in a similar fashion, seeking low-cost ways to increase supply in order to gain more benefits from high prices, while slowing down production when prices are low and buyers are few so that, again, only the lowest-cost units are attractive to produce.

Responsibility

Because they are voluntary, transactions in the marketplace do not take place unless each participant believes that he or she will be better off. This means that each market participant, unable to gain from trade without advantaging the trading partner as well, must attempt to reconcile his or her own goals with those of others. Negotiations, auctions, and other market means whittle away at waste as each participant tries to obtain the best deal. Buyers seek the lowest-cost source; sellers seek the highest-valued buyer. This process leads to the satisfaction of both parties if a trade takes place. And trades do take place, because each person is seeking something from the other. This arrangement is in contrast to a government situation in which one party can use coercion against others and thus can ignore these others' wishes.

The result is that in the private sector resources move to uses that have higher value—that is, a use that someone is willing to pay more for. A cattle rancher earning little money may find that more revenue can be gained by allowing wild elk to thrive, producing game for hunters. This is happening throughout the West. Deseret Ranch in northeastern Utah, for example, was losing money in the cattle business. The new manager, Gregg Simonds, had to figure out how to make a profit. Through the creative application of new ideas, he fostered elk on the property, increasing the herd size from 350 to 2,000, with benefits for many other animals as well, including bison, deer, mink, mountain lions, and beaver. By charging hunters for the opportunity to shoot trophy elk, Simonds enabled the ranch to start making money. He also improved the management of cattle, reducing feeding costs by raising the productivity of the grasslands (Anderson and Leal 1997, 79–82).

A private owner has an incentive to recognize and respond to the goals of those who want the products that the owner's assets can supply. Adding value means that more wants are satisfied even though other less intensely desired goals may be sacrificed. Through this process, everyone, or nearly everyone, in society is made better off.

The evidence for this improvement is the continually rising incomes in market economies. Market economies are more prosperous and grow richer than economies that rely more on government and less on market allocation of resources (Gwartney and Lawson 2000). The goals of each person differ, but generally rising incomes allow all or nearly all to satisfy more in the way of wants. Even in poor countries, the poorest part of the population sees their incomes rise at least as fast as the economy as a whole (Dollar and Kraay 2000).

This process of seeking mutually satisfactory outcomes challenges private owners to be innovative in finding ways to increase the value and productivity of a resource. Change is always painful, and as some skills and some other resources become less valued, their owners must adjust. Nevertheless, the history of market economies shows that even those least advantaged do in fact prosper over time. Furthermore, in the private sector the cost to those working for constructive change is normally much lower than in a political system. Typically, the entrepreneur seeking to bring together key resources can obtain financing for a project by convincing only a few investors that the innovation has promise. Investors are eager to adopt plausible innovations because "the early bird gets the worm" in the form of profits. This characteristic of capitalism, in contrast to the need to convince the relevant majority in a democratically controlled agency such as the U.S. Forest Service, explains why nearly all new technologies developed and adopted in the past century have come from nations with capitalist economies (McCracken 1987).

By contrast, political decision makers personally have little to gain by taking a chance on an innovation. They will be reluctant to pay the personal costs needed to take the initial risk and push for an innovation until it has a proved track record or broad backing by voters. In theory, nothing prevents government from being innovative; but because the battle is harder and the rewards are smaller for the entrepreneur in the government setting, innovation is much less frequent than in a competitive market setting. A dramatic illustration is the technology that was used in the Soviet Union: "One cannot look about Warsaw or Moscow, Budapest or Zagreb, Krakow or Sarajevo without knowing that this part of the world is caught up in a technological time warp," wrote W. W. Rostow in 1991 (Rostow 1991, 61). There are nonmonetary rewards for innovation in both the private and the public sectors such as personal satisfaction and recognition, but in the private sector these rewards are powerfully augmented by the hope of profit.

THE FUTURE

Perhaps the most dramatic contrast between governmental and private control is the difference in the way each affects the future use of resources. Property rights provide long-term incentives for maximizing the value of what is owned. This is the case even for owners whose personal outlook is short term.

The current worth of any asset or resource reflects the value of the future services it can provide. The owner of land has a strong incentive to maintain its value because any perceived reduction in its future services reduces its market value today. The reverse also is true: any new and better way of producing more value in the future increases the present value of the asset. Property rights give owners the privilege as well as the responsibility of control. Thus even a short-sighted owner has the incentive to act as if he or she cares about the future usefulness of the land. This incentive applies to vigilance in avoiding potential liability for damages. It applies even if the land is owned by a corporation, and the corporate officers, rather than the owner-stockholders, are in control. Corporate officers may be concerned mainly about the short term, not expecting to be present when future problems arise. But property rights hold such decision makers accountable. If certain actions are expected to cause problems, or if current expenditures are seen to promise future benefits, the stock price captures the reduction or increase in future net benefits (Jensen 1986; Kensinger and Martin 1988). Property values and stock prices change with expectations of future profits and losses, even though the current profit-and-loss statement may not reflect the results of bad decisions and good investments for years to come.

Results of Market Mechanisms

Those living in a society that relies on private ownership and protects resource owners against theft and invasion (including pollution) gain several benefits. One is the increased value of resources because they are used more efficiently (less wastefully) and because they are used in ways that are increasingly valued by those in the society. There are two other benefits:

Cooperation. Private efforts to find gains do not destroy the social fabric in the way that conflict over alternative uses of government resources does. Because government-owned resources are "up for grabs"—that is, subject to continual reallocation—many people get involved in conflicts over what to do with them. It is useful to contrast the experience of the National Audubon Society with respect to the Alaska National Wildlife Refuge, on the one hand, and the Rainey Preserve, on the other.

The Audubon Society is adamantly opposed to drilling for oil on even a small portion of the Arctic National Wildlife Reserve in Alaska. "A wildlife refuge is no place for an oil rig!" says its literature. Yet the Society allows companies to drill for natural gas (and a small amount of oil) on its preserves, most notably the Rainey Preserve in Louisiana (Baden and Stroup 1981, Snyder and Shaw 1995). This seeming contradiction is explained by the fact that one is government-owned and one is privately owned. At Rainey, though the goals of the Audubon Society and the oil company are quite different, the two sides maintain a calm and cordial atmosphere as they negotiate over what sorts of preservation might be accomplished while drilling occurs. Both sides find that they can gain by listening sympathetically and thinking creatively about new and better ways for each to get what it wants at minimum cost to (and thus minimum price demanded by) the other side.

This cooperative negotiation occurs because each party realizes that insisting on an extreme position would mean no agreement and no trade, so that each would have to give up potential benefits that could be offered by the other side. Both sides find that if they can bargain calmly and refrain from defaming the other side, they can each gain from exchange. In the political arena, however, discrediting the opposition by defaming them and inflicting similar harms can actually pay, since most voters know little about the real situation and are susceptible to claims by both sides, each saying that the desires and the proposals of the other are illegitimate.

Diversification of risk.   Another benefit of market control is diversification of risk. This reduces the exposure of individuals in the society to dangers caused by inevitable human mistakes. In the private sector, the risks are diversified because, instead of all the resources in society being committed to a single, agreed-upon course of action, there are many diverse ideas, all of which may be acted upon at the same time. The less successful ones are quickly abandoned, as and when the investors discover their mistakes. Investors do not want to throw good money after bad by continuing on a mistaken path. After all, their own resources are at risk.

Consider grazing land in the United States today. The federal Bureau of Land Management owns millions of acres, many of which are leased to private owners. It is the policy of the BLM to limit the number of cattle or other livestock that may graze on these acres, and the limits have been going down year by year in response to concern that the range may be overgrazed. In contrast, some innovative ranchers, including the manager of the already mentioned Deseret Ranch in Utah, have adopted a technique somewhat like crop rotation. Instead of reducing the impact of grazing by reducing the size of the herds, the ranch encourages intensive grazing by large herds on a small piece of land for a short period of time during the spring. The herds are then moved to another parcel of land. By winter, grasses have returned to the pasture in sufficient quantity to support the cattle for the winter season (Anderson and Leal 1997, 81). The idea is to mimic the action of the bison on the Great Plains many years ago. This radical departure from traditional wisdom has been adopted by some ranchers, but not by all. With a government-mandated system, only one approach is typically allowed. Under such a system, the traditional BLM approach of strict limitations on the number of cattle allowed might have prevented this alternative from even being tried.

Government mandates (at least on the national level) tend to put all of the society's eggs in one basket. Even though experts are involved, political pressures decide the issue, and the general public interest has no strong and well-organized constituency. Because government decisions have a broad impact, the results can be disastrous. For decades, it was the policy of the National Park Service and the Forest Service to suppress fires on millions of acres of government-owned land. That policy, which allowed the buildup of dead and dying trees, has created tinder for enormous wildfires that periodically cut a swath through our parks and forests (Nelson 2000, 15–21).

The diversity that nearly always occurs in "chaotic" markets is a powerful antidote to this "one size fits all" situation. Indeed, producers and consumers alike benefit from the proliferation of ideas and innovations. The losses from unworkable ideas are borne by the private innovators whose decisions prove to be wrong—not by the other members of society, as occurs when a government decision is in error. Like the many unsuccessful mutations in remorseless nature, human planning failures in the private sector tend to be quickly weeded out as owners try to avoid further losses. Successful innovations are copied, of course, wherever they work.

To understand the broad scope of private protection of the environment, one must recognize that the private sector includes nonprofit organizations as well as profit-making ones. Many nonprofit organizations have an important role in conservation. For example, land trusts, which are private nonprofit organizations that preserve land, are proliferating in the United States. Before 1950 there were fewer than forty; by 1998 there were 1,200 (Land Trust Alliance 1998). The largest organization of this kind is the Nature Conservancy, which purchases land to protect critical habitat and

preserve watersheds. These organizations use the tools of the marketplace to achieve their objectives.

Many nonprofit environmental organizations were formed in
direct opposition to public policy at the time (Council on Environmental Quality 1984). The Hawk Mountain Sanctuary in Pennsylvania, for example, was created to protect hawks and other birds of
prey at a time when the state of Pennsylvania, consistent with the
advice of established wildlife biologists (including those supporting
the National Audubon Society), had a bounty on certain kinds of
hawks because they ate other birds. Governmental protection of
hawks would have been impossible. Today, many years later, the
project is reversed, and government agencies seek similar goals.

Liability

The benefits cited above occur with a completely private system.
They support the view that private property rights can counter the
problem of the commons. But not all commons can be privatized.
Air (and to a large extent water) is unlikely to be privately owned.
Thus, the usual choice is to bring the government in to control
emissions into air space and bodies of water.

Historical evidence shows, however, that a system of private
ownership can reduce environmental pollution of air and water
through the tradition of common law. This follows from the fact
that pollution usually damages other resources (sometimes including human health), not just the quality of the water or the air.
When the courts uphold the rights of people whose property is
being harmed or whose health is being damaged, protection against
pollution through court suits has often been quite effective. Thus
the common law reduces the problem of the commons even without requiring formal ownership of air or water.

In England, there is a private right to fish for trout or salmon, a
right owned initially by the landowner adjacent to the water (but

transferable to others, including individuals or clubs). As a result, long before there was a politically effective antipollution movement, the private owners of fishing rights took polluters and potential polluters to court. They forced them to refrain from polluting streams in ways that hurt fish and thus violated the rights of fishing rights owners (Shaw and Stroup 1988).

The ownership of fishing rights is a distinct and effective right, but the common law protects air and water in other situations as well. History is replete with evidence that people whose land or water was harmed by polluters were protected through the courts in the United States as well as in Britain (Meiners and Morriss 2000). As a result of these court decisions, polluters, whose wealth was also at stake via liability exposure, took action to prevent future court cases. Some installed water pollution control devices. Wisconsin paper mills recognized in the nineteenth century that they were liable for harm caused downstream by effluent from the mills. They bought up large areas of land so that the effluent would be sufficiently diluted by the time it reached others' property (Davis 1971). This may not be a satisfactory solution today, but at the time it was an effective way to prevent harm to others from the pollution.

Although federal control has to some extent superseded common law protection against pollution, lawsuits still have a role in protecting against pollution damage. Ownership of the air or the water is not necessary for the enforcement of the right to be free from damage by contaminants.

Private lawsuits cannot, of course, correct all environmental problems. Some involve just too many polluters and too many victims—as in the Los Angeles basin, where air pollution is caused by the exhaust from thousands of automobiles whose owners are, of course, among the victims of the pollution. The basin is truly a commons, abused because chemical wastes (such as partially burned fuel) are dumped into it.

Even so, when they can, parties whose wealth and livelihoods are at stake are more likely to take effective action in dealing with pollution control than is a civil servant in charge of a similar government asset. In the United States, where the government owns the fishing rights (as well as the water in streams),[6] there was no action to stop stream pollution as there was by the anglers and others who owned fishing rights in England (Shaw and Stroup 1988). State departments of fish and game, which had responsibility to protect water quality, seldom used their standing in courts to do so. Rarely were the waters or the fish protected as they were in Britain.

Some environmental issues resist a market solution even more than does the problem of air pollution in Los Angeles. Protecting the ozone layer, which helps keep out excessive ultraviolet radiation from the sun, from potentially destructive chemicals is difficult to solve through markets. Protecting the world's population from excessive buildup that might occur through excess carbon dioxide production also would be difficult to solve privately. Government policy in this difficult case may be no better. Since good public policy is a commons, achieving a responsible policy may be impossible.[7] Evidence comes from the governments that have been bargaining over how to carry out the Kyoto Protocol, which is designed to reduce carbon dioxide emissions to slow global warming. Political forces—national governments and multinational companies among them—are more interested in jockeying for trade advantage for industries and firms in their nations than in attempting to reach efficient levels of harm reduction and in levying equitable costs. One observer reports:

6. Actually the government agency is trustee for the people, who themselves "own" the resource. As trustees, however, they have much the same rights as an owner when it comes to protecting the streams and the fish against polluters.

7. The problem of properly directing government to serve the general public effectively is discussed more thoroughly in Stroup (2000).

. . . some countries, such as the United Kingdom, are positioned to exploit carbon reductions they have made in the past by raising the cost to economies that still rely heavily on coal. Other countries, including developing countries and some European nations under one proposal, are allowed higher emissions. They see opportunities of payments from the developed countries for reducing carbon emissions or for offsetting actions such as planting trees. (Yandle 1999)

More important to these negotiators than the future impact of carbon dioxide are the present political and economic distribution of the treaty's short-term effects.

Finally, even though some problems seem intractable through markets, the lack of property rights does not mean that a useful property rights solution is forever impossible. Property rights tend to evolve as technology, preferences, and prices provide added incentives and new technical options. Early in American history, property rights in cattle seemed impossible to establish and to enforce on the Great Plains of America. But the growing value of such rights led to the use of mounted cowboys to protect herds and eventually to barbed wire to fence the range. The plains lost their status as commons and became privatized (Anderson and Hill, 1990). Advances in technology may yet rescue schools of whales in the oceans, migratory birds in the air, and—who knows?—even the global atmosphere, if that is needed.

CONCLUSION

In sum, private ownership and the market process, when they can be adopted, make resource owners and users accountable for costs they incur and reward them for value produced. The record of market economies over the past two centuries confirms the benefits of replacing the commons with private property rights and markets. Not only are such nations consistently more prosperous, they also have better environmental quality. A growing literature has shown the environmental benefits that come from economic prosperity and, more specifically, from the protection of private property rights. Higher living standards, longer life expectancy, and freedom from water-borne diseases occur more rapidly under private ownership (Norton 1998) and market economies typically pollute less than socialist ones (Bernstam 1995). By these measures, succeeding generations are better off under private ownership.

In addition, natural resources are better protected under systems of private property rights (see, for example, Deacon 1995) and they are becoming cheaper, not more expensive, for each succeeding generation (Simon and Kahn 1984). The loss to future generations as a consequence of the harvest of natural resources, including non-renewable resources, has been more than overcome by investments in capital facilities and technical knowledge and in human health advances. Today our economy has fewer ore bodies rich in minerals, but the minerals that the remaining ore bodies produce cost less to obtain. In sum, few of us would, on sober reflection, choose to live in the past, however much we romanticize it.

Hardin's key insight in "The Tragedy of the Commons" was that we must expect decision makers to be focused on narrow, perhaps even selfish, interests, and that this implies the need for an institutional framework that leads them to act as if other resource uses, and other users including those in the future, are also important. For the sake of our environment as well as our prosperity, the way to accomplish this is through a system that, wherever possible, relies on markets rather than on governments.

REFERENCES

Anderson, Terry L., and Peter J. Hill. 1990. "The Race for Property Rights." *Journal of Law and Economics* 33, no. 1: 177–98.

Anderson, Terry L., and Donald R. Leal. 1997. *Enviro-Capitalists: Doing Good While Doing Well.* Lanham, Md.: Rowman and Littlefield.

Avery, Alex, and Richard Halpern. 2000. "What Are We Paying These Guys For?" *Regulation* 23, no. 2: 6–7.

Baden, John A., and Richard L. Stroup. 1981. "Saving the Wilderness: A Radical Proposal." *Reason.* July.

Bernstam, Mikhail S. 1995. "Comparative Trends in Resource Use and Pollution in Market and Socialist Economies." In Julian L. Simon, ed., *The State of Humanity*, pp. 503–22. Cambridge, Mass.: Blackwell Publishers.

Breyer, Stephen. 1993. *Breaking the Vicious Circle: Toward Effective Risk Regulation.* Cambridge, Mass.: Harvard University Press.

Chase, Alston. 1986. *Playing God in Yellowstone.* Boston: Atlantic Monthly Press.

Coase, Ronald. 1960. "The Problem of Social Cost." *Journal of Law and Economics* 3, no. 1 (Oct.): 1–44.

Council on Environmental Quality. 1984. *1984 Annual Report of the President's Council on Environmental Quality.* Washington, D.C.: U.S. Government Printing Office.

Davis, Peter. 1971. "Theories of Water Pollution Litigation." *Wisconsin Law Review*, pp. 738–816.

Deacon, Robert. 1995. "Assessing the Relationship Between Government Policy and Deforestation." *Journal of Environmental Economics and Management.* January, pp. 1–18.

Dollar, David, and Aart Kraay. 2000. "Growth Is Good for the Poor." World Bank. Downloaded July 18, 2000, from: http://www.worldbank.org/research/growth/absddolakray.htm.

Economic Staff. 1980. "Descriptive Analysis of the Data from the Bryce Canyon National Park Visitor Survey." Unpublished report, Office of Policy Analysis, U.S. Department of the Interior, Summer.

Fretwell, Holly Lippke. 1999a. *Forests: Do We Get What We Pay For?* Bozeman, Mont.: Political Economy Research Center. July.

————. 1999b. "Paying to Play: The Fee Demonstration Program." *PERC Policy Series* PS-17. Bozeman, Mont.: Political Economy Research Center. December.

General Accounting Office. 1999. *Western National Forests: A Cohesive Strategy Is Needed to Address Catastrophic Wildlife Threats.* GAO/RCED-99-65. Washington, D.C. April.

Goklany, Indur M. 1996. "Factors Affecting Environmental Impacts: The Effect of Technology on Long-term Trends in Cropland, Air Pollution, and Water-related Diseases." *Ambio* 25, no. 8 (Dec.): 497–503.

————. 1999. *Clearing the Air: The Real Story of the War on Air Pollution.* Washington, D.C.: Cato Institute.

Gordon, H. Scott. 1954. "The Economic Theory of a Common Property Resource: The Fishery." *Journal of Political Economy* 62 (April): 124–42.

Gwartney, James D., and Robert Lawson, with Dexter Samida. 2000. *Economic Freedom of the World 2000 Annual Report.* Vancouver, B.C.: Fraser Institute.

Gwartney, James D., Richard L. Stroup, and Russell Sobel. 2000. *Economics: Private and Public Choice.* Fort Worth: Dryden Press.

Hardin, Garrett. 1977 [1968]. "The Tragedy of the Commons." In Garrett Hardin and John Baden, eds., *Managing the Commons*, pp. 16–30. San Francisco: W. H. Freeman. Originally published in *Science*, December 13, 1968, pp. 1243–48.

————. 1978. "Political Requirements for Preserving Our Common Heritage." In H. P. Brokaw, ed., *Wildlife and America*, pp. 310–17. Washington, D.C.: United States Government Printing Office.

————. 1993. "The Tragedy of the Commons." In David R. Henderson, ed., *Fortune Encyclopedia of Economics*, pp. 88–91. New York: Time, Inc.

Jensen, M. C. 1986. "Agency Costs of Free Cash Flow, Corporate Finance, and Takeovers." *American Economic Review* 76, no. 2: 324–29.

Kensinger, J. W., and J. D. Martin. 1988. "The Quiet Restructuring." *Journal of Applied Corporate Finance* 1, no. 1: 16–25.

Land Trust Alliance. 1998. *National Directory of Conservation Land Trusts.* Washington, D.C.

Leal, Donald R. 2000. "Homesteading the Oceans: The Case for Property Rights in U.S. Fisheries." *PERC Policy Series* PS-19. Bozeman, Mont.: Political Economy Research Center. August.

Leal, Donald R., and Holly Lippke Fretwell. 1997. "Back to the Future to Save Our Parks.: *PERC Policy Series* PS-10. Bozeman, Mont.: Political Economy Research Center. June.

Mankiw, N. Gregory. 1998. *Principles of Economics.* Fort Worth: Dryden Press.

McCracken, S. 1987. "Democratic Capitalism and the Standard of Living." In *Modern Capitalism.* Vol. 1, *Capitalism and Equality in America,* ed. Peter L. Berger. New York: Hamilton Press. (Esp. p. 16).

Meiners, Roger E., and Andrew P. Morriss. 2000. *The Common Law and the Environment: Rethinking the Statutory Basis for Modern Environmental Law.* Lanham, Md.: Rowman and Littlefield.

Mitchell, William C., and Randy T. Simmons. 1994. *Beyond Politics.* Boulder, Colo.: Westview Press.

Nelson, Robert. 2000. *A Burning Issue.* Lanham, Md.: Rowman and Littlefield.

Norton, Seth W. 1998. "Property Rights, the Environment, and Economic Well-Being." In *Who Owns the Environment?* ed. Peter J. Hill and Roger E. Meiners, pp. 37–54. Lanham, Md.: Rowman and Littlefield.

Pigou, A. C. *The Economics of Welfare.* 1960 [4th ed. 1932]. London: Macmillan.

Rostow, W. W. 1991. "Eastern Europe and the Soviet Union: A Technological Time Warp." In D. Chirot, ed., *The Crisis of Leninism and the Decline of the Left.* Seattle: University of Washington Press.

Shaw, Jane S., and Richard L. Stroup. 1988. "Gone Fishin'." *Reason,* August–September, pp. 34–37.

Simon, Julian L., and Herman Kahn. 1984. *The Resourceful Earth: A Response to Global 2000.* New York: Basil Blackwell.

Snyder, Pamela, and Jane S. Shaw. 1995. "PC Oil Drilling in a Wildlife Refuge." *Wall Street Journal.* September 7.

Stroup, Richard L. 1991. "Controlling Earth's Resources: Markets or Socialism?" In *Population and Environment* 12, no. 3: 265–84.

―――. 2000. "Free Riders and Collective Action Revisited." *Independent Review* 4, no. 4: 485–500.

Viscusi, W. Kip, John M. Vernon, and Joseph E. Harrington, Jr. 1997. *Economics of Regulation and Antitrust.* Cambridge, Mass.: MIT Press.

Wolf, C., Jr. 1988. *Markets or Government?* Cambridge, Mass.: MIT Press.

Yandle, Bruce. 1999. "Bootleggers, Baptists, and Global Warming." *PERC Policy Series* PS-14. Bozeman, Mont.: Political Economy Research Center.

CHAPTER FOUR

Tragic, Truly Tragic:
The Commons in Modern Life

Ronald F. Lipp

"RUIN IS THE DESTINATION toward which all men rush, each pursuing his own best interest in a society that believes in the freedom of the commons. Freedom in a commons brings ruin to all." In this succinct and striking epigram, Garrett Hardin in 1968 limned the essential conflict between individual liberty and the common good famously known as the "tragedy of the commons." Hardin's seminal essay,[1] which has launched a thousand dissertations and other academic papers, saw tragedy in the solemn remorselessness by which well-intended private actions work public ruin. The particular commons he had in mind was the communal pasture, open to all to use as they will, with no herdsman burdened to bear the cost of its maintenance. In his own natural self-interest, each grazes as many cattle as possible, reaps his private profit, and thereby assures that over time the pasture falls into decline, taking with it the collective fortunes of the herdsmen, their families, and community who depend upon them.

1. Garrett Hardin, "The Tragedy of the Commons," *Science*, December 13, 1968, pp. 1243–48.

HARDIN'S TRAGEDY

Although Hardin's immediate example was communal cattle herding, he saw real-world parallels as diverse as ocean fishing, parking on public streets, and recreation in public parks. The tragedy shared by all is the degradation of productive capacity or other utility. But Hardin also saw a reverse model in the problem of pollution, the dumping of sewage, chemical, radioactive, and heat waste, and noxious fumes into the air and water. Each of us, in our actions as independent, rational, free enterprisers (Hardin's term), contributes to the fouling of our collective nest. For Hardin, the problem of pollution is even more vexatious than the loss of productive capacity:

> The tragedy of the commons as a food basket is averted by private property, or something formally like it. But the air and waters surrounding us cannot readily be fenced, and so the tragedy of the commons as a cesspool must be prevented by different means, by coercive laws or taxing devices.[2]

Thus, he was led to propose "mutual coercion, mutually agreed upon by the majority of the people affected."

Hardin's prescription, founded on deep distrust and fear of individual action, is one of coercive intervention, politically imposed, to supplant private activities and the rights of private property with collective action or control. Over the last thirty years, this has been the prevalent paradigm in the United States and influential elsewhere in the control of environmental hazards and, to a lesser degree, in management and regulation of access to "public" resources.

Before considering the evident breadth of Hardin's concept and the expansion and dilution to which it is naturally subject—a prin-

2. Ibid., p. 1245.

cipal topic of this essay[3]—it may be useful to articulate the essential elements of the model and of Hardin's proposed solutions. As expressed in Hardin's illustration of the communal pasture, the commons classically portrays a specific arena in which particular individual actions taken in the pursuit of private objectives bring tangible, discernible, incidental damage to the public, usually in the form of degradation of the utility of the commons or of environmental damage. The commons is presented in models such as Hardin's as a ground of being, that is, a venue in which actions, causality, and effects are discernible and measurable—must be if the calculus of injury and redress is to be done. And the calculus must be done if the remedy of mutual coercion is to be imposed, since the legitimacy of public control depends on demonstration of its superiority to the preceding state of individual freedom. Certain crucial, if seemingly trivial, elements of that calculus are worth noting: the damage to be demonstrated and avoided is injury to the *public* welfare, political coercion may be resorted to as a solution only insofar as the insufficiency of a regime of private property can be demonstrated, and the determination of the good must take into account the interests of everyone affected by the commons. On this last point, Hardin himself acknowledged that individual interests were not to be ignored because of some more important public interest; we are obliged to weigh *all* interests, including individual and subjective ones, and to show that coercive intervention creates the optimal benefit compared with the available alternatives with all those interests taken into account.

3. This essay is a preliminary and provisional exploration of commons as a social and ideological phenomenon, a topic to be more fully developed in a larger future work.

THE COMMONS APPLIED

Recognition of the tension between private interest and public welfare in respect of goods held in common, or public venues in which benefits are encumbered by their correlative burdens, did not originate with Hardin. The observation that men are most attentive to their private interests to the detriment of those held in common goes back at least to Aristotle,[4] and the related problems of externalities, free riders, and public goods have long been a staple of economic analysis.[5] This cluster of issues is often characterized as a question of market failure, or more pejoratively a failure of capitalism. It is an important feature of Marxist analysis and is the most important source of economic arguments for government intervention in the marketplace. In addition to environmental protection and conservation, such diverse areas as education, traditional municipal services, and other goods thought subject to natural monopolization (such as telephone, electrical, and postal service) have figured prominently.[6]

---

4. The usual citation to Aristotle is *Politics*, 1261 30–37. In the century before Aristotle, the Athenian historian Thucydides made a similar observation. No doubt this human characteristic is so fundamental that a search of ancient literature would find earlier sources in a variety of cultures. Thucydides remarked that "[T]hey devote a very small fraction of the time to the consideration of any public object, most of it to the prosecution of their own objects. Meanwhile, each fancies that no harm will come of his neglect, that it is the business of somebody else to look after this or that for him; and so, by the same notion being entertained by all separately, the common cause imperceptibly decays." *The History of the Peloponnesian War*, bk. I, sec. 141.

5. Some sense of the vast literature on this and related topics may be gleaned from the *Encyclopedia of Law and Economics* (http://inprem.rug.ac.be/~gpremer/encyc/). Under "Category 2000 Common Property: General Theory (incl. Common Property Versus Private Property)," some 600 publications are listed; this compilation is not exhaustive, nor is this the only pertinent category in the *Encyclopedia*.

6. For an excellent compilation of essays examining economic and philosophical arguments with respect to public goods, see Tyler Cowen, ed., *The Theory of Market Failure: A Critical Examination* (Fairfax, Va.: George Mason Uni-

The law has a long tradition of intervention to restrain private behavior in these core areas, whether by command-and-control regulation, nationalization of private firms, or exclusive reservation of the arena for government action (for example, military force and criminal justice). Not all these interventions are grounded in economic analysis. Most have some component of communitarian justification.[7] In Roman times, the Emperor Justinian established a series of things thought common to everyone as a law of nature: the air, running water, the seas, and the seashore. In the Anglo-American legal system, the public trust doctrine provided a common right to pass through navigable waters; today, that doctrine serves in many jurisdictions to provide a right of access and use to submerged and submersible lands for public use and navigation. Efforts are under way to expand the public trust doctrine in radical ways, including the protection of recreational activities and public rights to "view sheds."

Over time, traditional economic rationales such as Hardin's for intervention to control or supplant private conduct have been narrowed and undermined by analyses of several sorts. Some scholars have found that the historical foundations of approaches like Hardin's are faulty. It turns out that many historic "commons," including medieval pastures and perhaps even Native American hunting ranges, were not in fact commons open to indiscriminate use but involved complex and sophisticated regimes of private rights of utilization that effectively prevented Hardin's anticipated tragedy. The ingenuity of traditional societies in creating systems of private

---

versity Press, 1988). For an interesting overview of public goods and externalities, see David D. Friedman, *Price Theory* (Cincinnati: South-Western Publishing Co., 1986), pp. 412–28.

7. A recent development in which traditional communal rights have been newly asserted to overcome established private property interests is found in *Nansay Hawaii v. Public Access Shoreline Hawaii*, 903 P.2d 1246 (Haw. 1995), *cert. denied*, 517 US 1163 (1996).

rights has been followed by modern development of new forms of property or property-equivalents that have in many cases eliminated or at least circumscribed the justification for government intervention (for example, transferable pollution permits and privatization of hunting and marine fishing rights with the correlative right to manage game and fish as a natural resource).[8] Similarly, covenants and other contractual restraints and consensual quasi-private social arrangements have proved useful as a substitute for coercive governmental action.[9] In addition, government intervention has been discouraged by expanded judicial insistence that compensation be paid for governmental takings of private property.[10]

Skepticism about the efficacy of compulsory interventions in management of the economy and in environmental protection has also resulted from growing awareness of the uneven historical record of public management. The breakup of the Soviet bloc in 1989 and of the Soviet Union itself in 1991 brought to public light for the first time in both East and West comprehensive evidence of the dismal record of resource management by the former Communist regimes. These states, supposedly dedicated to public welfare and in possession of nearly untrammeled authority to compel private behavior, nearly everywhere produced nightmares of air, water, and soil pollution, economic waste, and impoverished public health. This devastation resulted from both the core ideological values of Communism and the lack of practical accountability of the bureaucratic cadres to the publics who were the supposed beneficiaries of the system. The failure of government planning on a

8. See Edwards et al., *Conservation Through Commerce: A Roundtable Discussion* (Washington, D.C.: Center for Private Conservation, 1998).

9. See Burlin et al., *Conservation and the Public Trust Doctrine: A Roundtable Discussion* (Washington, D.C.: Center for Private Conservation, 1999).

10. See *Nollan v. California Coastal Com'n.*, 483 U.S. 825 (1987), and *Dolan v. City of Tigard*, 512 U.S. 374 (1994). The seminal work in this area is Richard Epstein, *Takings: Private Property and the Power of Eminent Domain* (Cambridge: Harvard University Press, 1985).

large scale has obvious implications for government planning on a small scale, particularly today when interventionists propose expansion of the role of governments into vast new areas of human activity.

Although the record of governments in the West has been vastly better than those in Communist and other socialist states, there has nonetheless been widespread disillusionment with schemes of social engineering, such as the War on Poverty and various welfare programs, and with government economic regulatory programs. Even in the West, governmental actions have resulted in some of the worst environmental mishaps.[11]

EXPANDING THE COMMONS

In spite of the developments traced above, which have constrained traditional justifications for intervention, the commons remains the prevailing paradigm, nowhere more than in the public's imagination. That fact has tempted interventionists to try for more, to move from concrete, practical, and specific cases of economic production and ecological risk to more abstract and ephemeral economic and environmental cases. Once upon a time, government intervened to protect neighbors from the stench and other effluents of a local abattoir. These days it proposes to protect their stakes in the global atmospheric envelope.

In some sense our "environment" reaches far beyond even the

11. For example, the inadvertent introduction into the United States of the chestnut blight in the 1930s by the United States Department of Agriculture resulted in "the largest single change in any natural plant population that has ever been recorded by man." S. L. Anagnostakis and B. Hillman, "Evolution of the Chestnut Tree and Its Blight," *Arnoldia* 52: 3–10, quoted in J. R. McNeill, *Something New Under the Sun: An Environmental History of the Twentieth-Century World* (New York: W. W. Norton, 2000), pp. 255–56. McNeill's treatise is a wide-ranging examination of the effects of human action on the environment in the past century.

most extended issues of economic production and traditional forms of pollution. In his seminal essay, Hardin also attacked the "evils of the commons in matters of pleasure" and complained of "propagation of sound waves in the public medium" by such offenses as "mindless music" in shopping malls, the noise of supersonic aircraft, and the aural and visual pollution produced by radio and television advertising. Indeed, ultimately, the "environmental" problem extended to the intolerable claim that each human makes on the commons by asserting his freedom to breed; Hardin proposed to put a stop to that.[12]

But why stop there? Doesn't the true elasticity of the concept extend to any aspect of life in which large numbers of people seem to share some characteristic or value? Lest it be forgot, Aristotle's original observation about the natural tendency of men to attend to their individual interests and neglect those held in common was a rejoinder to the vision in Plato's *Republic* of a society in which communal spouses and children would replace traditional familial relations. Aristotle knew, as Plato apparently did not, that the loss of direct kinship and individual connection would result in a loss of affection and care. But their dispute suggests that all human relations are indeed fair game.

Nor have we yet plumbed the concept's limits. Hardin and Aristotle focused upon the dolorous effect on the human community arising from individual action in the commons; Hardin and his kindred justified the diminution of personal liberty on the basis of the net utility to that community. But an even broader view of the commons seeks to restrain human activity in the name of another—nonhuman—community. The utilitarian argument is thereby fundamentally subverted: humanity as a whole must impose a net loss

12. Hardin's Malthusian dread of overpopulation as the ultimate tragedy of the commons was not, of course, his own original insight. In his 1968 essay, Hardin credited an early nineteenth-century pamphlet by William Forster Lloyd, *Two Lectures on the Checks to Population* (Oxford: Oxford University Press, 1833).

on itself for the good of something else whose claim to well-being takes precedence. The argument once invoked to justify individual suffering for the greater good of us all now ratchets up to compel our collective misery. Thus, some environmentalists have advanced a value theory according to which the well-being of nature needs to be considered for its own sake, with other species protected— even at the cost of net human loss—on the ground that humans have no particular claim of privilege.

THE SUBVERSION OF ANALYSIS

Something quite important is afoot here; the very nature of the commons is in flux. In the classic model, the commons under scrutiny is either demonstrably a "commons" or self-evidently so; the nature of the activity in question and the consequent harm are sufficiently concrete and specific to make analysis possible and useful. The real focus of examination is the attempt to find and weigh solutions. Can the commons be privatized or something like private rights created? Can individual behavior be modified by consensus or consent? Should the commons be regulated by command and control or perhaps nationalized? At what costs and to what benefit, and in each case to whom? As the model is expanded to cover ever more difficult, uncertain, and conjectural cases, our capacity to identify these factors and perform the necessary calculus looks more and more doubtful. It soon seems apparent that the model, when expanded, has also become diluted from a robust analytical tool into an affective or sentimental tag. But in fact, these hard cases simply reveal a defect in the model that has always been present in even the simplest cases of the model.

To seek the common good is a daunting task; to understand and value the particular interests of affected individuals is equally so. Skepticism about our capacity in even the most prosaic cases should be heightened by recognition of the great difficulty commonly experienced in reaching agreement about goals even in instances of voluntary associations. Such voluntary collectives as homeowners associations, partnerships, and corporations with fairly concrete and focused collective objects—preservation and enhancement of the neighborhood or operation of a profitable business—typically require elaborate, detailed specifications of the collective purpose, the relationships among participants, and modes of dispute resolution. And these are often thought to be ineffective—as, for example, excessive compensation of corporate executives is often asserted to be imperfectly related to shareholder welfare—and frequently lead to litigation or other forms of dispute resolution. If we are challenged to identify the common goals of small groups gathered for narrow purposes, and forced to recognize how many individual, conflicting goals swim in the collective soup, how much more difficult is it to determine the common interest in larger and more amorphous arenas?

Take, for example, the air we breathe. We are told that we share a common interest in clean air, one of the essentials of life. To be sure, there is some minimum quantity of oxygen and maximum quantity and type of pollutants that constitute thresholds for maintaining human existence. But beyond that, what? The eighty-year-old person surely has a different stake in the preservation of air quality than the infant. The asthmatic, the athlete, and the sedentary bookworm have different requirements. And although we "all breathe the same air" euphemistically, we don't in fact. Residents of Medicine Lake, Montana, and central Los Angeles breathe quite different air, and they may have quite different views of draconian measures to diminish auto emissions that also increase the cost of fuel and vehicles. Besides, there is more than health at stake. You, living in the central city, may hate the haze and odors in which you are immersed, whether they impair your health or not; I living in the countryside to the east love to sit on my back porch with a glass of wine at the end of the day admiring the gorgeous sunset, even though I know that its ruddy glow is in part an unintended consequence of your pollutants. I enjoy being a free rider.

Even Hardin recognized the inherent difficulty of utilitarian calculation:

> We want the maximum good per person; but what is good? To one person it is wilderness, to another it is ski lodges for thousands. To one it is estuaries to nourish ducks for hunters to shoot; to another it is factory land. Comparing one good with another is, we usually say, impossible because goods are incommensurable. Incommensurables cannot be compared.[13]

For Hardin, the solution to this Gordian knot was the sharp blade of science in service of necessity:

> Theoretically this may be true; but in real life incommensurables are commensurable. Only a criterion of judgment and a system of weighting are needed. In nature the criterion is survival. . . . Man must imitate this process. . . . The problem for the years ahead is to work out an acceptable theory of weighting. Synergistic effects, nonlinear variation, and difficulties in discounting the future make the intellectual problem difficult, but not (in principle) insoluble.[14]

Of course, this assertion of faith in the prospect for "scientific management" of society is not a new idea. Nor is the impossibility of the solution thus proposed.[15] By suggesting that man must imi-

---

13. Hardin, "The Tragedy of the Commons," p. 1243.

14. Ibid., p. 1244.

15. Calculating the "ideal" air quality and the "optimal" means to achieve it by government operation or control seems to be nothing more than a particular application of the Marxist program of managing an economy without market pricing to allocate resources. In 1922, Ludwig von Mises demonstrated in his classic *Socialism* the impossibility of economic calculation in the absence of a market pricing mechanism. Nothing in the intervening years has undercut his demonstration of the intellectual bankruptcy of command-driven systems. A good survey of the debate on this question appears in Michael Wohlgemuth, "Has John Roemer Resurrected Market Socialism?" *Independent Review*, Fall 1997.

tate nature in selecting survival as the sole and single criterion, Hardin repudiates his earlier acknowledgment that all subjective and individual values must be embraced in the calculation; it is no doubt because, as Hardin also acknowledges, "It is not mathematically possible to maximize for two (or more) variables at the same time." In fact, it is difficult to avoid the conclusion that the suggestion of accounting for all values is anything more than a sop. It is impossible to imagine the calculus and the basis for weighing all the subjective incommensurable preferences in even a modest regulation of the commons and even in some approximate way—about as impossible as it is disagreeable to imagine the regulatory process that would attempt to substitute some monolithic alternative. Inevitably, coercive control of the commons will sweep away all individual, subjective values and placate the dominant actuating impulse of whatever pressure groups are of greatest influence. In our times and culture, that will assuredly mean the subordination of other values to health and safety claims, with an occasional seasoning of feel-good sentimentality that vows to save the whales, the rain forest, the earth, or whatever.

Such sentiments are no doubt often sincere and admirable, but they risk substituting bumper-sticker epigrams for serious analysis. At worst, they evoke some graphic image of horror that has the effect of stopping discussion.

In a recent work, His Holiness the Dalai Lama says, in a discussion of universal responsibility and industrial pollution, "Imagine the pollution of an extra two billion cars."[16] The Dalai Lama is an extraordinary man deeply engaged with the suffering of the world and rightly deserving the great respect and even reverence that he is accorded. His teachings merit our sincere and serious consideration. But I wonder if his statement was intended to provoke deep

16. His Holiness the Dalai Lama, *Ethics for the New Millennium* (New York: Riverside Books, 1999), p. 166.

analysis or to shock us into insight, much in the manner of a Zen koan. I would prefer to take his question literally and to examine the circumstance he suggests. One's first image, I suppose, is of a world made gray and gritty by a dramatic leap in airborne emissions and soil and water contamination, with a resulting decline in human health and the world's well-being. Surely such a development is undesirable and should be stopped or at least controlled by compulsion to protect the fragile envelope of the world. But I wonder if all, or even most, would agree.

The number of automobiles in the world is something on the order of one-half billion.[17] The addition of another two billion represents a fourfold increase. At present, the developed world, with a small fraction of the planet's human population, uses the bulk of its automobiles. It also has a mature, largely saturated automobile market and a low and apparently declining birthrate. It seems highly likely, therefore, that most of the additional autos will go to less prosperous and developed portions of the world, that, say, four billion relatively poor persons will acquire most of the two billion automobiles. Since, as we imagine the automobiles exist, the world's economies must have found the means to produce them, and since it seems unlikely that a vast increase in auto consumption would be chosen while housing, food, and health care remain at poverty levels, it also seems likely that these new autos augur correlative improvements in those goods and services and, necessarily, the infrastructures to support them. So, it appears that the Dalai Lama has imagined a world in which the global capacity to produce wealth has grown so vastly as to bring the majority of the world's now struggling populace to the level of at least the less wealthy developed nations, say Greece or Portugal. One may also speculate

17. According to the *Encyclopedia Britannica*. For reasons of comparability of data, my illustration does not take into account trucks, but there is no reason to believe the inference is impaired by that omission.

whether that increase in the capacity to produce wealth would not itself generate the means to reduce or offset much of the pollution that this scenario imagines. But even without that speculation, ask yourself this: if the average Ukrainian or Pakistani or Nigerian were given a choice between his present life and one in which he could provide his family with the means to live on a level approaching the West, but at the price of greater pollution, which would he choose? To pose the question is to answer it.

But we have been speaking only of the interests of all persons now alive in respect of an existing condition. If, instead, we hold the world in common, as trustees for the good of future generations, how are we to know their true interests? If we hold as trustees for others than humans, for whales or rats, how do we possibly acquire the godlike prescience for that task? If humans of, say, Herman Melville's generation had impoverished themselves by preserving whales as a source of future illumination, they might be surprised to learn that electric lamps have entirely supplanted that need. To suppose that whales or rats should be preserved for nature's benefit supposes an even more astonishing predictive capacity about the desirable course of natural development and about the relative costs and benefits. Evolution, even in the absence of human intervention, constantly alters the number and balance of species. If we arrest the influence of human society, do we have any evidence that the evolutionary course of the world will be improved? Shall we reintroduce *variola major* into the natural environment and curtail our efforts to suppress *yersinia pestis* and *treponema pallidum*—and consider the consequent epidemics of small pox, plague, and syphilis simply to be part of our "dues" for maintaining the natural order? And which natural order: the array of species which existed at the beginning of 1999? 999? 10,000 B.C.E.?

THE COMMONS IN METAMORPHOSIS

We have seen the concept of the commons eroded in two ways: by its extension into ephemeral areas in which causation and effect are problematic and by the subversion of human interests to antihuman ones. The first change extinguishes whatever utility the commons has as an analytical tool. The second throws it into ethical confusion by substituting radical and alien new objectives for old ones widely agreed upon. One might expect that these changes would be the death of the concept. But, paradoxically, these infirmities seem not to have curtailed the model's appeal but to have liberated it from restraint, creating something new: the commons as metaphor, a symbol with so powerful an emotional appeal that it serves as a kind of icon or talisman. The current agenda of interventionists is truly vast and nebulous: the purity of oceans, of the world, and the air we breathe; the preservation of nature, Spaceship Earth, Gaia, the Cosmos; the holiness of life. We are speaking of fundamentals, our heritage not simply as humans but as beings. Surely, we sense, we must hold such universal, elemental things "in common." And if so, how can we say that claims made on behalf of other beings are less compelling than our own? The mind is stunned. How exactly to test these claims—of whether, how, and in what respect our interests are indeed common and of what priority human interests have over others—is difficult to say. These vast, dreamy issues are of such scope and of such compelling emotive power that it somehow becomes almost seditious even to ask. Better just to yield and let the question go. The assertion of commons is no longer the starting point of analysis; it is the end.

THE COMMONS AS ICON

We now see Hardin's commons inverted, transformed from the ground of being that supports analysis of interests that are to be reconciled into a metaphor, or really an icon, that serves and often is intended to thwart the analytic process. Hardin's tool has become its opposite, the commons as talisman. I use the terms deliberately—metaphor, icon, even talisman—to identify a symbol of great emotive pull with a kind of magical power, whose invocation trumps reason, analysis, and factual inquiry. This phenomenon is a larger, older, more ubiquitous, and far more dangerous one than Hardin's model could ever be in its own right. The point of the preceding discussion was to show the capacity of the former to become the latter so the full potential of its harm might be seen.

All processes of abstraction, generalization, and analysis involve the creation or use of categories that identify and distinguish common characteristics. They are essential tools of cognition and analysis and the essence of induction and deduction, requiring only that they be recognized as useful artifices and not confused with reality. "All other things being equal": but in fact they never are. This is the case of Hardin's herdsmen. Of course metaphor may serve as a useful shorthand in analysis and as a handy rhetorical device. It is ubiquitous in our cultural discourse in both guises; allusions to the American way, the Black community, the Jewish experience are useful to link some subject group with some shared core of values or experience. If that's all that happens, fine; no harm, no foul.

But as metaphor, those reservations, statements of conditions, assumptions, and limitations of analysis are apt to be forgotten. Metaphor is therefore inherently dangerous; allusion necessarily loosens our attachment to reality. That is its purpose, the very thing that makes it useful. But if sufficiently detached from the assumptions that define its limitations and remind us of its quality as artifice, the metaphor of commonality risks being invoked as a mythic symbol or religious icon, asserted as a matter of faith or direct revelation, not only unsupported by factual proof but offered as immune from the necessity of proof. How much easier for an advocate to raise a call to arms by invocation of an emotionally powerful icon that galvanizes his constituency than to resort to the tedious business of persuasion by reliance on reason. It may even be that if you demand proof in the face of such a symbol, you prove yourself disqualified to receive it. Women's way of knowing; men just don't get it.

There surely are some things that groups such as the elderly, Blacks, Jews, and women experience in ways common to each other in some degree and different from others in some degree. But those observations quickly lead to sharp distinctions between groups and at the same time submerge differences among individual members of any group. Thus, Blacks in general may have suffered from racial discrimination, and so civil rights advocacy may appeal to the insult and injury suffered to the Black community. But a young, upper-class Harvard-educated Black male may well have more in common with his Jewish or "Wasp" counterpart than with a poor, uneducated Black octogenarian woman. References to the reactions of the "Black community" (or to any other) thus contain a large potential for hyperbole—and dangerous hyperbole when the assertion of communities of interest leads to calls for action. As with other commons, interventionists will arise who will claim to represent the community and to act for the supposed benefit of the commons whose individual members are said to be unable to act for themselves.

As the symbolic power of a particular claim of commons rises, so do the risks of challenging it and the benefits of being coopted by it. If Thomas Sowell, a Black academician, makes the assertion in the preceding paragraph, he risks being ostracized as disloyal; if I, who am not Black, make that assertion, I risk being accused of racism. In times of political turmoil, these risks may be intolerable. To be called un-American, racist, sexist, or an "Uncle Tom" could at various times imperil livelihood and even life and limb. At the same time, a powerful metaphor creates great benefits for those who are able to secure inclusion within the protected community.

The symbol may therefore be self-perpetuating for as long as the underlying sources of its power persist and even after they have dissipated. During popular wars, the strength of patriotism and the risks of being thought disloyal strongly motivate a country's residents to subscribe to the patriotic mythos; and even after that impulse has largely spent itself, say when peace is well established, a strong residual impulse to observe rituals of allegiance may long remain.

The metaphor of commons can be equally compelling in defining a disfavored and despised group to which some dreadful defect or failing is attributed. Racial, ethnic, and religious categories, but also pejorative economic and social classifications are commonplace. "No Chinese or dogs allowed." "Scab-lover." The condemnation and even abuse of a disfavored group is likely to be exacerbated when a favored commons is projected in tandem. Groups need enemies; leaders of groups especially need enemies to spur the allegiance and efforts of their members. Devotion to the cause of the proletariat is furthered if bourgeoisie, counterrevolutionary, and imperialist enemies threaten everywhere. Domestic grievances may be muted if the plots by foreign devils, Jewish bankers, or even the "ruling class" can be offered as distractions.[18]

The power of the metaphor for interventionist purposes may be

---

18. It is common knowledge that class warfare was a central feature of Communist theory and propaganda. It is less commonly recognized that the same was also true of the Nazis, who, as in so many other respects, were the Communists' close cousins. Class warfare was an essential feature of German culture and was availed of by the Nazis early on. In 1920, the National Socialist party, in its first bid for public support, issued a manifesto called "Twenty-Five Points" that was filled with appeals based on class envy and differences. Point 24 raised the metaphoric commons to the level of universal principle by asserting that "our nation can only achieve permanent health from within on the principle: *The Common Interest Before Self.*" Under Nazi principles, a criminal was not one who violated individual rights but one who injured "the common interest." Leonard Peikoff, *The Ominous Parallels: The End of Freedom in America* (New York: Stein and Day, 1982), pp. 190–92, 196.

strengthened by the fluidity of the asserted classification. In American civil rights experience, the class of "minority" has been sufficiently plastic to include women (a numerical majority) and to exclude Japanese and Chinese Americans, a distinct numerical minority (for example, in college admissions, where they excel). Sexual deviance has contracted to exclude homosexuals but expanded to include those who engage in "unwanted touching." In contemporary American political culture, the categories of "the disabled" and "victims" thus far know no limits. Even seemingly concrete, fact-based classifications are capable of opportunistic manipulation. In Nazi Germany, the category "Jew" went beyond any rational basis of ethnicity, religion, or culture. In the Soviet Union, emotional cover for Stalin's program of rural terror and collectivization during the 1930s was provided by a campaign against the "kulaks," a supposed class enemy of the revolution. The term had some historical pedigree as a vague referent to rich peasants or usurers, but the class of kulaks as class enemies was created by Stalin from whole cloth. At the outset, it was said to constitute the upper strata of landed farmers, but with each wave of the campaign, it was redefined to include whoever remained who possessed any property not yet confiscated or was simply identified as an opponent of the regime.[19] In Western political experience, the categorization of the "rich" or "wealthy" has enjoyed a similar creative freedom in the hands of those who would impose taxes or controls.[20]

19. Martin Malia, *The Soviet Tragedy: A History of Socialism in Russia, 1917–1991* (New York: Free Press, 1991), pp. 196–97; Paul Johnson, *Modern Times: The World from the Twenties to the Eighties* (New York: Harper Colophon Books, 1983), pp. 270–71.

20. Tax collections, and claims to future revenue based upon the existing tax system, are a peculiar commons that results from government command and control. When private wealth is converted into tax revenue, it is detached from and no longer accountable to the citizens contributing it. The fund thus becomes a kind of government property unburdened by private claims, which accounts for

As a powerful symbol that is divorced from and immune to analysis, the metaphoric commons relentlessly benefits from and in turn promotes the suppression of attention to individual differences, in both favored and oppressed classes. Individual members tend to be objectified and dehumanized; the symbol is thereby further insulated and protected from any test of its veracity or relationship to reality.[21]

In the polar case, the commons is untethered from any test or criterion except its ability to satisfy a clientele that believes its ideology. If we who are labeled Volk or proletarians believe that we are vexed by Jews or capitalists, we will support the programs of our leaders. Even if we disbelieve those claims, we may support those programs for the gains, albeit ill gotten, we receive or to escape being ourselves labeled traitors or Jews or capitalists.

The true clientele of such a commons will in time cease to be the community and become instead its leaders and their minions. No system has demonstrated this development more fully or clearly than the various Communist regimes that have afflicted the past century. None has more audaciously based its use of power on the assertion of service of the common interest. What is most compelling about the Communist example is its adherence to the same model across many generations and cultures and always to substantially the same effect. And what is most remarkable about that effect is the way in which, even in the more mature and relatively benign stages of the regimes, the commons was subverted to the gratification of its political class.

---

not only the tenacity of government retention of tax revenue but also the apparent belief of government bureaucrats in the legitimacy of their entitlement to it.

21. There is fertile ground and considerable need for consideration of the objectification involved in the metaphoric symbolism of the commons in light of modern psychological theories of internal object relations. For a survey and development of the latter, see Thomas H. Ogden, M.D., *The Matrix of the Mind* (Northvale, N.J.: Jason Aronson, 1990).

The origins and essential features of the Communist system are too well known to merit more than brief mention. The means of production, which ultimately entail virtually every aspect of life, are held by a class of professional politicians in the name of the class. The class is working people, common people, the proletariat, which ultimately elides to "the people," since all others are enemies and devalued. Since all belongs to the people, nothing belongs to anyone and custody over all must be exercised by the party cadres, in trust until the promised arrival of the mythical Eden of true Communism.

In a system that tolerates no rival power—no alternative commons or private autonomy—all depends upon the cadre and upon the actual efficacy of system. In time, as we know, the cadre of true believers is replaced by self-serving bureaucrats. And in time the existential defects of the system in delivering goods and services doom it to economic and social failure. In fact, its existential defects are such that the system's survival depends from the beginning upon hermetic isolation and a reign of terror.[22] In the end, after the most brutal aspects of the system have subsided, what remains is a kind of torpid dream. All pretense of belief in the system, whether by cadres or the people, has been replaced by an exhausted truce in which the latter acquiesce to leave the former in power and, in return, the former agree to leave the latter alone.

The final state, what Václav Havel has referred to as the "post-totalitarian" society, is illustrated by his famous parable of the

---

22. "[Communism] was in truth a 'tragedy of planetary dimensions'. . . the most colossal case of political carnage in history. . . . Communist regimes did not just commit criminal acts . . . they were criminal enterprises in their very essence: on principle, so to speak, they all ruled lawlessly, by violence, and without regard for human life." Martin Malia, "Foreword: The Uses of Atrocity," pp. x, xvii, in Stephane Courtois et al., *The Black Book of Communism* (Cambridge: Harvard University Press, 1999). For an in-depth discussion of these issues, see this volume generally, as well as Robert Conquest, *Reflections on a Ravaged Century* (New York: W. W. Norton, 2000).

greengrocer.[23] Among the goods displayed in his shop window, onions and carrots, the greengrocer places a sign bearing the slogan "Workers of the World, Unite." He does not do so because he believes it, or because he believes his customers or other passersby or even the political authorities believe it, or because he believes any of them believes he believes it, or because he believes anyone will be persuaded to believe it. He is, in fact, indifferent to the text. And it may even be important that he *not* believe the text, for there should be no misunderstanding that this ritual is a matter of belief, nothing to confuse the real message of his action in displaying it: "I know what I must do. I can be depended upon and am beyond reproach. I am obedient and therefore I have the right to be left in peace."[24] He, the victim of the system, thus secures his small oasis of solitude and thereby takes his place as an agent for the system's perpetuation. Even his superiors occupy the same position as both victims and transmission agents:

> [T]he inner aim of the post-totalitarian system is not mere preservation of power in the hands of a ruling clique. . . . [T]he social phenomenon of self-preservation is subordinated to something higher, to a kind of blind *automatism* which drives the system. No matter what position individuals hold in the hierarchy of power, they are not considered by the system to be worth anything in themselves, but only as things intended to fuel and serve this automatism.[25]

What Havel illustrates is a commons that has become its own end. If to Karl Marx "the human essence is the true collectivity of man" and, as Hegel taught, the collective whole lifts man to a higher sphere where, and only where, his true will can be realized, then the collective is more important than any man or even all men in

23. In Václav Havel et al., *The Power of the Powerless* (Armonk, N.Y.: M. E. Sharpe, 1985), pp. 23–96.
24. Ibid., p. 28.
25. Ibid., p. 30.

total except as they are one with the collective. The true end of the metaphoric commons is its own apotheosis.

For sheer viciousness of method and depravity of purpose, the Communist and Nazi regimes have no rivals. Yet, Western culture has not been immune from the use of the commons as a powerful icon to accomplish social engineering projects based upon some asserted ideal with punitive consequences for demonized, disfavored classes. One striking illustration is the Prohibition Movement in the United States, which culminated in the Volstead Act in 1920, following the adoption of the Eighteenth Amendment to the United States Constitution. It is well known that the Prohibition Movement was not only a campaign against a supposed health threat and social vice, alcoholism, but was also part of a larger war of virtue against sin. What is not always remembered is that this envenomed crusade (as it certainly was) was the talisman of an even greater struggle between culture and civilization and of middle-American nativism against Eastern cosmopolitanism. It was no accident that one of the leading spokesmen for Prohibition was William Jennings Bryan ("The Great Commoner"), whose program was populist and whose vernacular was anti-intellectual; nor was it accidental that the Prohibition campaign included open attacks on the "notorious drinking habits" of "immigrant working men."[26]

America's more recent campaigns against drugs, drunk driving, tobacco, firearms, and certain sexual activities bear the same hallmarks. Partly motivated to protect health and safety, they are clearly moral crusades in a vastly larger culture war. Their strength springs primarily not from the persuasiveness of their analytic case but from their emotive iconic power. These campaigns converge with another potent icon, the cult of victimization, which in our times is nearing its zenith. The salient characteristic of that phenomenon is the insistence that one has no responsibility for any of his own

26. Johnson, *Modern Times*, pp. 208–9.

shortcomings, while simultaneously maintaining that someone else must be to blame for them all. It thus couples the two dominant characteristics of modern culture: unfettered narcissism and global, unfocused guilt. Thus, in the tobacco wars, although the dangers of tobacco have been common knowledge since long before most current smokers were born (the pejorative term "coffin nails" has been applied to cigarettes for over a century; Webster's dates it to 1888), smokers are viewed as innocent victims of predatory tobacco companies, which must be punished with unprecedented punitive damages. On the other hand, smokers are themselves treated as pariahs, exposed to exclusionary practices that involve an element of humiliation. There are early indications that these campaigns will shortly extend to "junk foods," chemical additives, and biologically altered foodstuffs. No aspect of individual action is immune if intervention can be posited as a perceived threat to health or safety.

Thus, we are increasingly urged to radically restrict or circumvent private activity and market behavior in the development and use of genetically altered foodstuffs; in bioengineering involving new medical technologies, life support systems, organ harvesting, and reproductive cloning; in exploitation of the human and species genomes for an untold range of benefits; and in the free development of the Internet and other technological advances in access to and utilization of knowledge. The central tool of these forays is the assertion of the symbolic commons. Governmental control over access to and utilization by employers and insurers of information on genetic predisposition to illness and defects is thus not advocated simply on the grounds of privacy or contract relations; public control of human cloning, organ generation, and other aspects of bioengineering is not justified on the basis of discernible public health risks or of traditional concerns of criminal law but more broadly by appeal to the "common genetic heritage of humanity" and various scenarios of science-fiction-like doomsdays. The only difference between these appeals and earlier ones, such as the campaign to forbid the use of DDT or that to curtail nuclear energy, is that the new claims are so diffuse and remote as to resist any testing of actual causes and effects. As with the campaigns to control industrial and consumer activities in the name of global warming, ozone depletion, and species extermination, advocacy of intervention proceeds by a process in which the need for proof of specific effects and of the efficacy of particular interventions is commonly supplanted by appeals to fear and panic. It's too dangerous, we're told, to wait for the facts; we must do something and do it now.

The modern obsession with health and safety is grounded, however fancifully, in protection of human life. But as shown earlier, the commons as ungrounded metaphor ultimately has the potential to become self-justifying and to free itself from any rational program or even service to human welfare. One sign of this development is the emergence of the animal rights movement. This movement condemns as "speciesism" the notion that animals may be owned by humans, asserts that "owners" are no more than trustees who are obliged to observe the independent rights of animals, and, in its most extended form, asserts that humans have no precedence at all over other animals. The most prominent current representative of this position probably is Peter Singer, chair in bioethics of the Princeton University Center for Human Values. Singer has achieved notoriety for asserting, among other things, that it may be more compassionate to carry out medical experiments on hopelessly disabled, unconscious orphans than on perfectly healthy rats.[27] Although Singer's views are, by conventional standards, quite rad-

27. Singer's works include *Animal Liberation* (1975), *Animal Rights and Human Obligations* (edited with Tom Regan, 1976), *Practical Ethics* (1979), and *Embryo Experimentation* (edited with others, 1993). A recent profile of Singer suggests that he may be revising some of his more extreme views. Michael Specter, "The Dangerous Philosopher," *New Yorker*, September 6, 1999, p. 46. A useful general review of Singer's viewers is found in the on-line *Encyclopedia Britannica* (http://www.britannica.com/bcom/original/article/0,5744,3576,00.html).

ical, his books have been popular and influential and there is good reason to believe that "animal rights" is a popular movement in the early stages of achieving iconic status.[28] Once the commons is metaphorically divorced from an ethical grounding in human welfare, there is no reason that this, or any other scheme with sufficient emotional power in the popular imagination, should not succeed. To take Singer a step further, why isn't a focus on protection of animals just a further speciesism?[29] Why shouldn't we establish command and control regimes at a more amorphous level, to protect the biosphere, the planetary environment, and the "deep ecology" of life itself?[30]

THE PRESENT CHALLENGE

In modern times, societies everywhere have succumbed, in one degree or another, to the mass politics of iconography. This politics is made possible by (and in turn promotes) the ascendency of the class of professional politician, the development of techniques of mass marketing utilizing modern electronic media, and the continuing decline of firmly grounded ethical systems (coupled with their partial replacement by alternative spiritual systems, which often are

28. Early on, Singer sought to bring this movement within the same iconic space as the most successful movements in the civil rights area. Thus, chapter 1 of *Animal Liberation* is headed "All Animals Are Equal . . . or Why Supporters of Liberation for Blacks and Women Should Support Animal Liberation Too."

29. Singer is not alone in advocating subordination of human privilege. Joseph Sax has been prominent in urging the creation of an "economy of nature" in which all property is made subject to a natural right or trust managed by government supervision, establishing ecological limits to human behavior and giving priority to the rights of species (e.g., "eagles have a right to exist"). See the discussion and citations in Burlin et al., *Conservation and the Public Trust*, pp. 3, 15.

30. In another odd parallel between modern progressive causes and their totalitarian antecedents, Adolf Hitler, during the peak of his success, envisioned programs to forbid smoking, to make vegetarianism compulsory, and to establish special bureaucracies for the care of dogs and defense against gnats and insects. See Paul Johnson, *Modern Times*, pp. 381–82.

sympathetic to and even the sources of popular modern metaphoric causes). Its methodology is heavily influenced by and indebted to the stunning success of the regimes in Nazi Germany, Soviet Russia, and Communist China in the projection of idealistic symbolism (involving both deification and demonization) through vivid media imagery and by powerful emotive display.[31] Though their values may be quite different and their evocative quality less vivid and strident (in keeping with the more pragmatic nature of American character), the imagery of the New Deal, the New Frontier, the War on Poverty, and some of the moralistic campaigns mentioned earlier in this essay undoubtedly benefit from the New Soviet Man, the Great Leap Forward, and the Thousand Year Reich.

The dynamic of the mass politics of iconography is the identification by politicians and political activists of a putative commons identified with some group thought worthy of benefits because of some asserted suffering or deprivation, or some group deserving punishment or subjugation based upon some misconduct or undeserved windfall. Often both kinds of groups are conjured, one to play off the other. The acceptance of these classifications and the proposed action programs associated with them require a process of advocacy and persuasion involving the production of at least some real evidence of the asserted grievance coupled with some appeal to preexisting beliefs and biases to support persuasion. But the real goal is to move past demonstration and persuasion so that the imagery surrounding the commons becomes iconic, with images so emotionally resonating with the grievance and the offense that the program is self-actuating. Its mere invocation produces the reaction necessary to carry the program. The label of racist, anti-Semite, homophobe, bigot, sexist, chauvinist, or elitist carries in varying degrees such compelling emotional tags of a class of victims and a

31. Ibid., pp. 130–31.

class of oppressors as to supplant in many cases analysis of the charge and of the program intended as a remedy.

The scope of the modern interventionist agenda is truly vast and unprecedented. In some areas, these programs have already come to prevail. Public discourse on health and safety issues seems now largely to be a battle of metaphoric images. In others, particularly in environmental and biomedical arenas, there appears to be a steady progression toward adoption of a metaphoric model and to the success of those models in justifying new regimes of government intervention. The scope of these programs is so great that they have the potential not only to do harm in numerous specific arenas but to endanger the fundamental grounding of modern society in reality.

This is because of the way in which the commons interferes with—disrupts and strangles—the spontaneous formation of social order that is fundamental to the proper functioning, progress, and evolution of society. In the great historical example of the Marxist planned societies, government intervention in the administration of the commons not only interfered with the production and delivery of specific goods and services but also distorted the entire calculus of social functions. It did so by removing all judgments from any grounding in reality and by displacing the spontaneous process by which social decisions could be based upon millions of small, individual inputs based upon unique packets of knowledge and value. That is, it disrupted the market process in its broadest sense, an indispensable mechanism for accommodating the full range of human wants and needs. Despite the universal and dismal failure of the Marxist project, present-day social and political campaigns to control large and essential elements of social order, from issues of public health and safety to the evolutionary process itself, are an expansion of the metaphoric commons to ever more intangible and unmanageable aspects of existence vastly beyond the historic Marxist agenda. They threaten the same basic disruption of this crucial social mechanism.

There are some things that private action, whether in markets or other consensual arrangements, cannot do. There are some things that government must do, whether by direct operation or through regulation. And this is true despite the loss in the evolution of society by spontaneous action when private conduct is displaced by the doleful and uncertain unintended consequences that always attend public intervention. Fortunately, the number and range of genuinely necessary interventions is smaller now than it used to be. Not so very long ago, it was difficult to imagine that such basic functions as telephone and even electrical service could be provided privately or that airplanes and trucks could compete in the open market without rates and routes set by government decree. Everywhere, government control in the traditional arenas of economic activity is in retreat; even in traditional areas of environmental protection and conservation, alternative private solutions are everywhere emerging and being adopted. This sea change may be seen not only in individual markets but in the powerful devolutionary forces sweeping the globe, which tend to reinforce and amplify one another.

This transformation is possible because of technological change and advances in our understanding of economic theory, heavily reinforced by public disillusionment with past government interventions in the West in the name of public welfare and the massive failure of the programs of central planning in countries following the Marxist paradigm, both in the Communist bloc and in the so-called Third World. Paradoxically, at the very time that intervention in traditional economic functions is on the wane, there is a kind of metastatic explosion of appeals for government intrusion to supplant or regulate private behavior in new and more remote arenas. It is, to use a biological simile, as though the bacillus of intervention, having been subdued by the antibiotic of economic and philosophical analysis in the center, has rushed in a survival strategy to infect the periphery. And it seems to be no accident that the newly invaded cells are largely venues that are the least vulnerable to rational examination and analysis. These are arenas that are mainly influenced by appeals to fear, guilt, and mystical faith.

The great danger in the metaphoric commons is not only that it interferes with a reality-based discourse about what ought to be done in the face of any perceived threat or opportunity but that it interferes with discussion of how to act in each case—by private action in free markets, by voluntary agreement, by public regulation, or by direct government action. The great danger is the substitution of talismanic invocations for rational discourse. In an age when the baleful totalitarian ideologies of the twentieth century are finally being overcome, when the possibilities of human freedom and well-being have never been more apparent and the twin blessings and danger of technology and science have never been greater, it would be truly tragic if we abandoned individual liberty, rational colloquy, and personal autonomy as the foundations of social interaction and succumbed instead to the political correctness, newspeak, emotional manipulation, and mystical illusions of the metaphoric commons.

Václav Havel, who lived through the commons *in extremis*, described life within such a regime as the participation in a ritual in which appearances are accepted as reality:

> Individuals need not believe all these mystifications, but they must behave as though they did, or they must at least tolerate them in silence, or get along well with those who work with them. For this reason, however, they must *live within a lie*. They need not accept the lie. It is enough for them to have accepted their life with it and in it. For by this very fact, individuals confirm the system, fulfill the system, make the system, *are* the system.[32]

---

32. Havel et al., *The Power of the Powerless*, p. 31 (emphasis in original). From

In fact, it is impossible for appearances to be accepted as reality without their becoming reality. Whether in its full expression in Marxist society or as still ameliorated in Western consumer and industrial culture, the commons, however useful in its benign form, always contains this poisonous, destructive seed.

This is the true tragedy of the commons.

---

the vantage point of the post-Communist world, we may be tempted to dismiss such descriptions as having nothing to do with life in contemporary democratic Western societies. Yet, Havel saw his country to be "simply another form of the consumer and industrial society, with all its concomitant social, intellectual, and psychological consequences" (ibid., p. 27).

INDEX

PHILOSOPHIC REFLECTIONS
ON A FREE SOCIETY

A Series Edited by Tibor R. Machan

Business Ethics in the Global Market

Education in a Free Society

Morality and Work

*Individual Rights Reconsidered: Are the Truths of
the U.S. Declaration of Independence Lasting?*

The Commons: Its Tragedies and Other Follies